Global Fusion Music & Arts Books

WHISPERS IN THE MISTS OF TIME.
LOUISA LE MARCHAND

Louisa was born in the West Country in 1950. From an early age she became a prolific writer of poetry. At the age of twenty one, she moved to London where she felt that there were better opportunities to develop her creativity. She has been living and working in various locations there ever since.

A musician, TV producer, photographer, writer, storyteller, and poet, she now has a substantial body of work in variety of genre to her name. She has written, performed and co-produced three albums of her songs, including her most recent 'Jazzmoss', which has been described as 'poetic jazz'. Louisa collaborated with the multi-talented Ugandan musician Kaz Kasozi to produce this album and it includes performances by some of the top names in British Jazz.

Louisa believes that her poetry forms the foundation of her art. This collection 'Whispers in the Mists of Time', is a small sample from her huge collection of poems and has been long awaited by admirers of her powerful and original work.

Special thanks to;

Gill Swan, Lyn Beaumont, Ellen Jeffery, Mary Ball,
Kaz Kasozi, Freddy Macha and Frances Cumming.

Louisa Le Marchand

Whispers in the Mists of Time
A collection of poetry

Global Fusion Music & Arts
Books

Global Fusion Music & Arts Books

Published by Global Fusion Music & Arts 2008
Global Fusion Music & Arts, 55 Gurdon Road, London, SE7 7RP
Tel: ++44(0)2088589497
Email:globalfusionarts@yahoo.co.uk
Website:www.globalfusionarts.com

Printed in England by TG Print, London

ISBN-978-0-9560049-0-1

Artist details:
email:artistlouisa@yahoo.com
Website:www.artistlouisa.com

Global Fusion Music & Arts policy is to use papers that are natural,
renewable and recyclable products and made from wood grown in
sustainable forests. The logging and manufacturing processes are
expected to conform to the environmental regulations of the country
of origin.

Authors note.

I found it very difficult to decide on an order for the poems, whether I should order them by style, chronologically, thematically, or by some other category , but in the end I chose to arrange them alphabetically. I have been writing poetry for most of my life only beginning to keep any of my poems in the early eighties. They come to me in my quiet moments, moments of extreme emotion, or sometimes in dreams, so I feel that somehow they have a life of their own. Putting them in alphabetical order means that they are juxtaposed randomly and form their own piece of art, rather like a giant collage made up from different parts and times in my life. Although I am very fortunate to enjoy all of the many art forms I am involved with, poetry remains at the centre of my being. It has carried through dark and light, along my journey, I hope that you will find something that resonates with you inside these pages.

Louisa Le Marchand

Contents

A Call to Arms - 11
A Carpet of Yesterday's Tears - 12
A Child at Night - 13
A Crack in Humanity - 14
A Love Letter - 15
A Melanchony Moment - 16 & 17
A Psychopath and a Policeman - 18
A Portrait of Words - 18
A Prayer - 19
A Resurrection - 20
A Shadow - 21
A Soul Cleanser - 22
A Soul Without Direction - 23
A Tear for Birthdays Long Forgotten - 24
A Walk with Creation - 25
Across the Sacred Boundaries - 26 & 27
Alone - 28
Amour - 29
An Exclamation Mark - 30 & 31
An Identity of Spirit - 32
Art - 33
Birthday - 34 & 35
Birthday Gift - 36
Born Again - 37
Communion - 37
Creation's Tears - 38
Crick! Crack! - 39
Crystals of Eternity - 40
Death Won't Make an Appointment - 41
Debating with Myself - 42
Destiny's Wind - 43
Dinner Party - 44 & 45
Drowning in Music - 46
Dubb Rthythms - 46
Evergreens - 47

Everybody Has to Earn a Living Somewhere - 48 & 49
Fligree and Shadow - 50
For Whom the Bells Toll - 51
Fortune Tales - 52
From the Spent Embers of the Past - 53
Gift - 54
GOD - 55
Grief - 56
Happiness - 57
Heads up Asses - 58
I Stand Naked in the Grand Hall of the Mansion of Time - 59
In an Uncertain World - 60
In Fear of the Future - 61
In Lovers' Dreams - 62
In Others - 63
In Our Children - 64
In Our Dreams - 65
In Praise of Creation - 66
In the Chambers of My Heart - 67
In the Dream Court - 68
In the Eye of a Storm - 69
In the Solitude of Silence - 70
Is Love - 71
It's Hard - 72
I've Kept the Company of Darkness - 73
I Watch the Nightingale - 74
Just Words - 75
Learn to Play - 76
Life is a Carnival - 77
Look - 78
Look and You Will Find - 78
Moments of Inspiration - 79
Moon on the Water - 79
Moving Image - 80
Nana (my Grandmother) - 81
Nature's Treasured Jewel - 82
Night, Night - 83
Night Talk -84

Pathway - 85
Playtime in Life's Garden - 85
Questions - 86
Rebuilding - 87
Relations - 88
Responsibility - 89
Returning - 90
Rhythms of Africa - 91
Sailing - 92
Sculptured - 93
Sleep -94
Songs of the Universe - 95
Sonnet For Spring - 96
Sound - 97
Sovereignty - 97
Stepping nearer to Truth - 98
Storm - 99
Superiority - 99
Sweet Song for a Swallow - 100
Temples of Divinity - 101
The Battle - 102 & 103
The Bloodstained Inheritance of an Empire - 104
The Burdened Traveller -105
The Cannabis Man - 106
The Child Within - 107
The Circle is Complete - 108
The Creators Call - 109
The Dawning of a New Day - 110
The Last Doorway - 111
The Plumber from Plumstead Common - 112
The Postman and the Poltergeist - 113
The Price of Wisdom - 114
The Satirist Who Once Was King - 115
The Sea of Troubles - 116
The Struggles of a Lifetime - 116

The Worth of Words - 117
Through the Sunsets of Songs - 118
Tick Tock - 119
To Be English - 120
Tomorrow -121
Tomorrow Part 2 - 122
True Value - 123
Void - 123
Voyage - 124
Washing Over Me - 125
Where? - 126
When - 127
Where Consciousness Is - 128
Where Does - 129
Where Does it all Begin and Where Does it End - 130
Where is the Line - 131
Who Has the Most to Say - 132
Within Ourselves - 132
Words In Waltz Time - 133
Your Birthday - 134

Birth and death may be the beginning and the end, but what we do with the journey is what really matters.

Louisa Le Marchand 1997

A Call to Arms

The battle lines are drawn.
The call to arms once long forgotten.
The camouflage of our bodies hiding our true identities.

The forces of light and dark, stand, face to face.
Questions are asked,
Which side are we really on?
Can we ever really know,
Until,
The battle is in progress.
It began at the dawn of time and will continue into infinity.
We are a single soldier,
A pawn in the most powerful game of chess.
Led by instinct,
We face our enemy within.
Choices are made,
Conflicting interests.
Thrust and parry.
Guards are up.
Tensions rise like fire licking the funeral pyres of dead warriors.
The perfume of conflict hangs in the air.
We witness our own destruction and rebirth.
Symbols of chaos,
Spring up without the anticipation of expectation.
On going eye to eye encounters re-enforce our commitment.
Fear feeding on itself becomes an army of illusion.
Destroyed only by our belief in ourselves to stand and face this
courtier of darkness.
Dawn breaks,
Light and dark divide and lay in wait for the next confrontation,
The next call to arms.

A Carpet of Yesterday's Thoughts

Walking on carpets of yesterday's thoughts.
Casting of a cloak of thread bare reactions,
Housing the shackles of blinkered eyesight.
Faces of the unforgiving fading to back.
The struggle for identity purity lived and relived.
The perspective of decades changed through the filter of truth.
Jagged edges, smoothed by tears.
The smiles of children playing,
The laughter of women bathing in freedom.
The perfume of stillness.
The fragrance of understanding.
The light of a thousand sunsets shining,
Cascades of colour, prismed into eternity.
Visions of memories long forgotten,
Mirrored on the faces of ghost dancers, haunting the corridors
of circumstance with the apparitions of dead worlds.
Painted on a canvas of lies the poisoned longing of serpent
demons buried in a pyre of history's pages, leafed and closed
forever.
Walking on a carpet of yesterday's thoughts.
The many hands reach no more.

A Child at Night

As they lie asleep,
Aware only of a dream world.
I look upon their innocence with envy.
Faces depicting a restful sleep.
Cheeks rosy red.
The peaceful sound of a breath,
Life continuing its sustaining power,
Through the long night.
Storms come and go.
The ghostly hours pass with a haunting silence,
Broken only by an owl or a cat.
Their laughter, their tears,
Are yesterday's adventures.
Now they wait only for tomorrow's untold stories.
Then as the sun walks across the room
And chases away the night
Their little bodies awake, stretch, open eyes
And start a new day.
One that will never come again.
One dream world replaced by another.

A Crack In Humanity

The beckoning finger on temptation's hand lures you into
darkened places.
Down narrow alleyways that lead nowhere through doorways
that open into blackness.
Promises of heights not attainable.
Stimulation without effort.
No cause without effect.
A by-pass of reality.
Stranded in a cul-de-sac of despair.
Endless, soulless.
Motorways mile after mile.
Servitude to addictions pangs, the claws of illusion clinging to
our bloodstained flesh as it rips out the heart out of our
existence.
The beckoning finger on temptation's hand transforms,
Into the clenched fist of anger and hate.
Going nowhere and becoming nothing.
Like a corpse eaten away from the inside by the maggots of
self destruction.
The eyes that stare out lifelessly are connected to death alone.
A living death, held in temptation's hand.

A Love Letter

A love letter, a letter of love.
Words from heart to heart.
A deep felt feeling, emotions high.
Sentiments, conclusions.
A rose.
A kiss.
A journey.
A return.
The laughter as your eyes meet mine, the tears as we say
goodbye.
The words unsaid, the deeds undone.
But as you return, the joy will prevail and tears no longer fall.
United lovers kiss, hold and take a breath together.

A Melancholy Moment

My feelings of melancholy have no logic.
They are just my feelings. not bad, not good,
Just melancholy.

Looking inwards, feelings outwards, feelings.
Safe yet insecure, a warm yet chilled edge, sorrow, yet not
unhappy.
Being in touch with a tender, sensitive part of my being.
My feelings of melancholy have no logic.
They are just my feelings, not bad, not good,
Just melancholy.

A way of seeing my feelings through new eyes.
Experiencing my experiences through a new perception of
myself.
Listening to laughter with filtered hearing.
Seeing through tinted glasses.
My feelings of melancholy have no logic.
They are just my feelings. not bad, not good,
Just melancholy.

Tearful but not overwhelming, not in any accessible definition.
Somewhere between realities yet in a reality all of its own.
Sometimes unnecessary, sometimes very necessary.
Sometimes unrevealing, sometimes revealing everything.
My feelings of melancholy have no logic.
They are just my feelings, not bad, not good,
Just melancholy.

Some days melancholy can be counter productive.
Others prolific in its creative endeavours.
One person's melancholy can destroy another's.
Or rebuild a person and teach them to know part themselves
where they can feel, see and touch.
My feelings of melancholy have no logic.
They are just my feelings, not bad not good,
Just melancholy.

A rhythmical activity were consciousness expands.
No one asks for melancholy, no one even understands or
knows when it will appear.
Its just a moment of melancholy.
My feelings of melancholy have no logic.
They are just my feelings, not bad, not good,
Just melancholy.

A moment of melancholy.

A Psychopath and a Policeman

A psychopath in a cycle path resorted to violence.
When a pedestrian psychiatrist said that he was
insane.
The psychopath in the cycle path grabbed the pedestrian psy-
chiatrist
And demanded he eat the words he had just said.
The pedestrian psychiatrist begged his forgiveness
And said he would never say it ever again.
A passing policeman with paranoid problems,
Asked the psychopath in the cycle path if he was ok.
The pedestrian psychiatrist demanded,
That the passing policeman with paranoid
problems,
Take the psychopath in the cycle path and lock him away.
After nodding and winking and secret hand shaking,
The passing policeman with paranoid problems
Took the pedestrian psychiatrist and locked him away.
The psychopath in a cycle path and the passing
policeman with paranoid problems,
Now visit the pedestrian psychiatrist whenever they can.

A Portrait of words

I access my reality through a portrait of words.
Conceive photographs of dialogue on a canvas of sentences.
Paragraphed songs, form chapters of colour.
I play the music of creation.
Painting my story in a book of poetry.
Pixels of understanding on a landscape of verse.

A PRAYER

I watch your malady consuming you.
The fluctuation, slight moments of light,
Fading to grey.
And in the darkened hours, your fears engulfing you.
Holding on to your breath.
This most powerful of forces, as we enter this world.
You cling to your consciousness.
The laughter of times past, no longer with us.
Your energy drained.
I pray to my creator.
The being whose power, sustained the universe.
Whose hand has guided and held me,
Through my close encounters with death
And along my lonely path.
Please heal this person of light.
My chosen companion.
Pour down on her your healing power,
Bathe her in your love.
Bring back the joy to her heart, help her to wake into tomorrow
And leave the debris of the past behind.
Wash her soul with your light
And let her know your power and wonder.
Help her to trust in you and believe in her self.
Love, I call on you to heal my love.

A Resurrection

I feel sadness,. a deep sadness rising from
somewhere even deeper than I can recall
The pain it brings as sharp as barbed wire,
or splintered glass.
I know not the source of this pain, nor the reason for this
sadness,
Just its longing to be set free.
My own dark shadows drawn out by the shadows of others.
Singing with one voice they commune in discordant
disharmony, a banshee choir of misery.
On this Easter Sunday I resurrect my own suffering and crucify
myself with the hatred of others.
The guillotine tongues and poisoned arrow eyes of bygone
times, drawn up from the bile of my unconscious self.
The pox of unchristian values bursting out of the purulent boils
of inhumanity.
I must force this overpowering consumption of emptiness back
to its quagmire home, deep inside my being and raise up
myself and my consciousness once again to higher and higher
visions.
Perhaps one day I will be strong enough to do battle with
these demons.
To defeat my enemies both past and present.
But for now I am weary and wish to see the sun once more
and bathe in the white light of the creator's love.
So on this Easter Sunday I will resurrect my soul in the spirit of
my life's journey, in search of truth in the companionship of
love.

A Shadow

A shadow walks across my soul ,
Like a cloud across the moon,
Or the moon across the sun.
Eclipsing my very being and shutting out the light.
For these moments I am in darkness, my day becomes night.
All reason implodes on itself.
Flocks of uncertainty come home to roost.
Time stands on its end and is elongated.
A chill wind fills the space that was once warm and calm.
Light is on the outside and darkness takes centre ground.
Confusion reins supreme.
A shadow walks across my soul.
Momentary madness takes my breath away.

A Soul Cleanser

We use cleansers to clean our skin and free it from makeup
and the dirt of the day.
But what of our soul, what will cleanse the spirit from daily
grim,
Or re-hydrate our inner being?
Where can we find the deep moisturiser to revitalize the light
within us?
It may not wrinkle or show the signs of aging that our bodies
do.
But through neglect we disown it and allow the world's
illusions to take its place,
Like a child forever young,
Forever in need of our love and attention
It craves our recognition
And we in return crave its light and love.
It is a doorway to the infinite.
A mirror, revealing true beauty.
We deny its presence, we deny ourselves.
Ageless.
Pure and made from the most natural of ingredients,
Love.
As we remember and commune with this most important part
of ourselves,
It in return will cleanse and wash away lifetimes of impurities.
Walk in the shadows,
Or run free in the light.
Keep our spirit free.

A Soul Without Direction

A soul without direction is like a ship cast adrift mid-ocean,
without compass or radio,
Dependant on the transient, volatile nature of the elements,
Unable to communicate with others
Totally alone and unsure.
A soul with direction, has the universe to guide them
And the unity of creation to commune with.

A Tear For Birthdays Long Forgotten

I mourn the passing of a year and shed a tear for birthdays long forgotten.
Of empty moments and party filled rooms.
Of lonely days with shadow memories and curtains drawn to sunrise laughter.
A look, the clink of glass or hugs of fond remembrance.
Decades gone, faded into the past, like a breath caught in a breeze at twilight.
Whispers kiss on lips of steel and passion's fire gone cold.
The artist's eye closed in a blink, the depths of feelings felt.
Emotion distilled in vat of time served up with iced reality.
Sentenced by the judgements of the unforgiving and imprisoned by my own guilt of existence.
I now revel in the happiness and peace that I have worked for.
Give thanks for the gifts of the talents now revealed.
I mourn the passing of a year and shed a tear for birthdays long forgotten.

A Walk with Creation

Today I walked with creation.
I held her hand and breathed deeply the fragrance of her
presence.
Her light sparked and illuminated the gossamer treads,
Tapestries across the fallen leaves of autumn.
Rainbows danced along these fine silken fingers,
whilst swarms of moths pirouetted, caught in the sunlight,
hanging as if in performance.
The cosmic puppeteer gracefully moving each small player in
perfect time.
The sun with bowed humility coloured trees spoke volumes of
enlightenment.
The wind whispered.
Rustling up delicate rhythms in a myriad of percussive
precision.
I stared in awe at such beauty motionless for a while,
Unable to think only to bathe in this wondrous gift.
Today I walked with creation I held her hand and breathed
deeply the fragrance of her presence.

ACROSS THE SACRED BOUNDARIES

Across sacred boundaries the darkness creeps, like a mist
engulfing a graveyard its, oil like nature thick and dark.
Dripping into our lives from our earliest childhood the cloaked
figure, darkened shape that creeps up the stairs and crosses
the unspoken unwritten boundary between right and wrong
friend and enemy, father and abuser.

As children at play we cross each others boundaries,
Discovering and rediscovering each other until treachery
forced on by the darkness reveals itself to be ever present.

As we labour from employment to employment we observe
and then are drawn into the tantalisation of greed and lust.
We begin to steel, first time and then what ever is felt justified
or necessary, until the realisation that this is a boundary that
may be the thoughtless exploitation in reverse.

In our relationships our assumed partners cross our sacred
boundaries of safety and devastate our landscape of delicate
flowers and destroy our perfume of colour with their stench of
purification, hatred and selfishness until we reach the point of
almost total submersion in the darkness of others and our very
soul is engulfed forever in pain.

But from this time of uncanny love we rise like a phoenix and
fly back into the light of our own existence. But even there in
the sanctuary and safety of our own bedrooms the darkness
moves in like a thief in the night or a burglar in the daytime
trespassing into our home across the sacred boundary of our
security so we and others cross the sacred boundary when,
unaware or not caring of the damage or the havoc and carrion
waste to the peace and tranquillity and innocence that lies
within the sacred boundary, but though we live through lifetime
of perpetrators enough to destroy the strongest heart we can
rebuild the sacred boundaries of our life and stop the repeating
pattern of abuse and abusers.

Victim and violator, building and rebuilding our light, our confidence our very essence, only to have it smothered and drained away by the darkness of others like a vampire sucking blood from a victim. For even the harshest desert where it would seem that life cannot possibly exist a flower will grow to prove the force of life, or the life force. It has the power to heal and redevelop itself into that being again and build those sacred boundaries and our own inner strength and wisdom, so strong so impenetrable that the darkness is just a memory excluded from our world of truth and love by a lifetime of building our own sacred boundaries.

Alone

Alone I walk this path of life,
Unfolding as a journey.
Companions come,
Companions go.
Each company has its learning.

With one door in,
And one door out.
Life the passage in between.
And no regretting what cannot be
Or what has never been.

The source within,
The source without.
We search with no direction.
Ask any soul who has lost the way.
Where is that inner connection?

Yet the one who knows,
Waits in the wings.
Until our need is clear,
When we step off the stage,
And turn to them
We lose all doubt, all fear.

From that point on,
We need never want.
For love, or peace, or glory.
When they unlock the door,
That leads inside.
We then begin our story.

Amour

What is it to feel love?
What is it to know love?
We cannot be complete without love.
We cannot really live without love.
Love is the deepest feeling.
Love is the strongest.
Love is the weakest.
Love is both the seed and the blossom.
Love is a bond that can never be broken.
Love can put wind to sail and sail to wind.
Love knows only love,
Therefore true love,
Is truth itself.

An Exclamation Mark

Changes are the full stops in our lives as we begin a new sentence.
Sometimes the sentence will end with a full stop and others with an exclamation mark! Or question mark?
A comma may appear as we take a breather, or temporary rest.
But then we continue on to finish the sentence.
Many sentences will join together, forming a paragraph.
These are the lager sections of our lives and to begin a new paragraph can be daunting.
But not as daunting as when we begin a new chapter and all the sentences and paragraphs draw to a close.
We embrace this new chapter but as we near the end of the book and reflect on the many chapters, sentences and words that have made up this book,
We see,
The beauty and the pain,
The sorrow and the joy,
The semicolons and the colons,
The paraphrases,
The links between chapters,
A story told in all its complexities of language,
Yet felt and experienced beyond the description of words.
As in the womb our preface and our birth the introduction.
The book we have written, where fact is stranger than fiction.
This volume, is one small volume in a collection of volumes, that is part of a library.
Yet this library is part of a huge collection of libraries,
All these libraries are part of one infinite library
And the chief librarian has read and continues to read every word as it is written.
Through this infinite library the librarian gains knowledge and understanding of what it is to write a single word, or to complete a sentence.

We may edit out sections of our story we dislike, but they will always remain in the library of life.

Our final full stop is not ours to choose, it may be half way through a chapter, paragraph or sentence.

But only the librarian knows how our story ends.

So we must write each word, complete each sentence as if it may be the one to have the final full stop.

An Identity Of Spirit

As a child I played in green fields and watched the river carry a leaf off to distant lands.
The butterflies delicately painted the landscape with their presence,
Blue skies caressed with soft clouds.
Yet in this idyll lay dark from the depths of time.
The cruelty of anger and injustice of abuse.
So I ran through golden wheat and climbed trees heavy with apples.
On the outside the sun shone always, but inside storms of despair, guilt, rejection and insecurity raged.
Through my existence an eternity of pain rained down on my orchid filled orchard.
Distorting the illusion and casting me out into the baron wasteland.
I've walked across the deserts of despair and felt the heat of hatred on my brow.
The rejection of others, has blown me over like a sandstorm and mirages of hope disappeared into nothing.
My parched lips have longed for the water of acceptance and my sun scorched body asked for the shade of love.
My tired blurred eyes long to look on others who are ready to see me.
As my soul has been my oasis, my heart has been my gauge, to test the temperature of other's true nature and understand.
In search of my true home.
My true childhood.
An identity of spirit.
Beyond body and mind and without the chains of my emotions to tie me down.
From this place of strength I can release the past, look for the future and stand firmly in the present connecting each breath with the foundation of being and build my life on the solid ground of truth.

Art

Art the expression of life.
Kindred to mankind.
Capturing both pain and beauty.
Time locked forever.
Sphere within sphere.
Moment on moment.
One drop on an endless ocean,
Elevated by innermost feelings.
Movement of body and soul.
Awakening sensitivity revealed.
For all to see.
Art.

BIRTHDAY

As I scan the journey that has become my life
And read the volumes that make up my existence.
I have taken many breaths since my first breath.
Have walked many steps since my first step.
Have spoken many words since my first word.

The paths have sometimes been treacherous
And my companions not always worthy of my affection
and trust.
But sometimes even in the thickest, darkest forest
Could be found a small flower,
To brighten and encourage me on my journey.
And in the prettiest meadow
There would lie in wait,
For the unsuspecting traveller
A deep and engulfing bog,
Ready to draw into its depths any passing stranger.

For nature, like people can be unpredictable.
Yet as we follow the river we surely find the sea.
So as we trust in the truth within ourselves to guide us,
We will surely find our own individual paths of learning
Rich and diverse,
Powerful, yet as subtle as the single petal of a flower.

As I reflect,
It seems that time is as flexible and as rigid as I allow it to be.
Yesterday seems to be as far in the past as my earliest
memory.
And a week becomes a year in a lifetime,
Moving so fast like the strongest wave crashing to the shore
and rushing back into the sea, pulling in on itself.
A cycle of highs and lows.
Until the balance of life turns full circle.

As there within the hurricane of life,
Is the eye of the storm.
So within my torrent of existence,
Is a stillness that has grown.
Like a small delicate sapling into a giant oak.
With a strength, knowledge and beauty.

Beyond my lifetime of changes and extremes.
Of pain and pleasure.
Of lifetimes within a lifetime.
Of gifts and burdens.
Of thoughts without actions.
And actions without consciousness.

Birthday Gift

I have a keepsake.
Given to me by the mother and father of time.
A gift I must cherish and protect.
A precious jewel beyond all diamonds or stones of beauty.
Wrapped in a special wrapping.
Packaged with loving care.
This gift is mine alone and only I can experience it.
I may share it with others.
But I may never be given another.
Only time will tell.
But I must love this gift and value it above all else.
This gift.
The gift of life.

Born Again

You tell me you are born again, taken up the Christian mantle,
Yet you wear Christianity like a coat, casting it aside when it no
longer fits you.
'God bless'
You retort, like a child reciting a rhyme.
And then stab me in the side with a smile of Christian joy.
You tell me you've been born again, as if once was not
enough.
And discovered the wonders of the father,
As if the mother does not exist.
You pour away your milk of human kindness and let it curdle
into cheese.
As you hold your rod and staff upright, you strike me without
remorse.
You tell me you've been born again, you've seen the light and
walked away from darkness.
Yet if others walk on separate paths, then you curse them as
the Devil.
The Sunday Christian ritual, will cleanse you of your sins and
take away your guilt.
But to give your love unconditionally, is not what you are
about.
You say that you've been born again,
Well once was more that enough for me this time around.

Communion

We serve our Gods and take the sacraments of our beliefs.
The blood and body of our convictions wafer thin and watered
down.
Crucified by the nails of materialism.
We crown our spirit in the thorns of maya.

Creation's Tears

As the frost on the bare winter bows of willow turn to fine
droplets of water.
Hanging like tears in the morning sunlight.
Reflected in the drops of water below.
Like echoes of summer.
The rays of sunshine dance to a wakening,
A chorus of nature's choir.
Caught in the sparkling of light,
Each droplet clinging to the fine willow, as would a child to it's
mother, when confronted by a stranger.
Soon the heat of the day rises and this moment passes.
An unseen, unknown moment in time.
Droplets of water, hanging, caught in a framework of beauty.
A nether world of Winter and Spring.
Night and day.
The rising of the sun
The droplets of water on willow.
Joyful tears in creation's eyes.

Crick! Crack!

Crick! Crack! My bones complain like Kit Kat.
Crick, have a break, crack, have a Kit Kat.
As the perspiration runs off my body,
Hardly a glow more a waterfall,
I reflect on the hitchhiker who has gleaned a ride on my body.
" Going my way "
"Sure, hop in,
I've never been one to see some one stranded ".
"I didn't catch your name?"
"Enza! "
"Oh is it an Irish name like Enya? "
" No, more Hong Kong or Chinese, very popular after the First
    World War ".
" What's your other name? "
" My first name, Oh Influ " .
" Interesting! Influ Enza - very cosmopolitan ".
Then, having gained entry under false pretences,
Wolf in sheep's clothing, the mayhem begins.
Like the unwelcome guest,
Who drinks your last carton of orange juice,
Runs up a high phone bill and is always in the bathroom
Just when you need to go,
Our unwelcome visitor saps our energy,
Cancels all our plans for the next week, or two
And makes sure that we are well acquainted with our bed.
But like all unwelcome guests,
It does outstay its welcome and we fight back.
"No, you can't use the phone, oh and by the way,
  If you are hungry, try Asda,
  They do a great breakfast, really cheap!
  Yes, this is the train, bus and plane timetable.
  My Aunt is coming to stay, so no room I'm afraid,
  Aunty Bi, Aunty Biotic, of course I prefer Homeo Path"
Inside, our armies muster and repel the invader
And the hitch-hiker moves on to another unsuspecting victim.
But my bones are still complaining,
Crick, have a break, crack, have a Kit Kat
Doesn't seem so bad though, at least they are mine!

Crystals Of Eternity

Like fragments of a broken glass,
We smash and fragment into a myriad of pieces.
Each going their own separate way,
Yet part of the whole, united in the knowledge of that, which
was joined.
Some journey far from the point of impact and remain,
Lost in unknown time and space.
Others stay close and are easily found.
The further we go from the centre,
The more dangerous we become to ourselves and others.
Alone we remain damaged and broken,
Separated from the feeling of oneness.
Seeing only the brokenness of others.
There then is a task beyond all comprehension.
To re-unite all the small shards of glass that make up the
whole.
As individuals we can be sharp and dangerous,
But united we become a thing of beauty a vessel to hold the
waters of life
And quench the thirst of a thousand deserts.
So as the creator drops the glass and watches as it falls and
breaks.
So too shall it be in creation's hand re-united again.
Smelted by the fiery passions of truth.
In others as in ourselves lay the crystals of eternity.

Death Won't Make An Appointment

Death won't make an appointment, or phone to see if it can call.
It wont ring at the door bell, or send a massage with a friend.

It likes to try surprises, to turn up unannounced.
To catch you whilst you are sleeping, or spring out at a turn or a bend.

It may wait a lifetime and stand there looking bored.
Or grab you before your life has begun, tormenting in its scorn.

Some of us expect it, others crave its presence.
But it's always unexpected and we are always unprepared.

It's not an easy job, taking life from within the living.
But someone's got to do it, it's a job that has to be done.

So we'll leave it to the most experienced, the one who knows it best.
And carry on regardless, oblivious, that we might be next.

Debating With Myself

As I dance around the extremities of madness
And look inwards in my voyeuristic way.
I recognise the mirror images staring out at me.
My paranoid self is murdered by my psychopathic tendency.
Inside myself washed up and high and dry with only my
manic-depressive self to keep me company,
I listen to the voices of my multiple personalities partying
together and become inebriated on my addictive personality.
All this time my feelings of inadequacies sit in the corner and
listen to my egocentric self, spout off meaningless jodrell.
The psychoanalysts have analysed and the psychiatrists have
left
So now to keep a balance I grow oak trees and listen to the
sound of my breathing.
As my heart pumps the blood through my veins,
My mind is left to mind itself.

Destiny's Wind

The tears I shed like cleansing rain on a hot summer's day,
Wash away the pain of past regrets and soak into my porous soul,
As does the precious droplets into the parched soil of drought or dry landscape.
Passioned emotions stir like fresh spring water refreshing and pure,
Bubbling up and gaining momentum into a fast flowing torrent.
Destiny's wind blows sharp across my bow and turns my sails to directions new, to undiscovered waters.
Dormant feelings burst into bloom and caress the senses with the fragrance of hope.
Longings are fulfilled.
Dreams become a reality.
As I shed the tears like cleansing rain and nourish my porous soul,
With love.

Dinner Party

I've met those who worship LSD, the Yen or the Dollar.
They drive BMW, Porsche or Range Rovers.
Some have their sacred shrines in Hampstead,
With their hallowed silk rugs on religiously clean maple floors.
One sits nervously in designer reverence on couches,
Hoping that none of your impurities will rub off onto their holy furniture,
Or some small speck of dust will fall from your impure non-designer clothing
Unto their Immaculate Conception dining chairs.
As you are in discourse with fellow financially spiritual dinner guests
On such philosophical subjects as interest rates and property prices,
Jocular merriment passes from one to another.
As the Holy Sacraments of the dinner are laid to rest
And the best port wine, Body and Blood of Christ,
Are passed to the left or is it the right?
To complete the ritual service.
One sits and soaks in the sheer awesomeness of
these giants of worldly mysticism
And stare in wonder at their ability to discuss
in such depth and understanding
On some of the great mystics of our time:
Bill Gates, Margaret Thatcher, The Convergence of the European Community.
I add my small irreverent confessional contribution
By drawing attention the lilies
Set so creatively in the centre of the long rain forest table on a third world mat
And say, "Isn't the Creator incredible?"
To which the worshippers retort,
" Who are they, a French designer?"
And look from one to another and ask,
" Do we have any of their designs?
Probably one of those Far East copies
Still I made a handsome return on my investments there last year."

Soon we all perform the last rites

Kiss, Kiss,
"Super darling!"
"Fabulous!"
"Yes I'll phone!"

I walk into the still small hours
And stare at the stars
And the beauty of the moon, caught in a cloud.
A fox ambles its way down a quiet street
And I say to myself,
" I wonder whose label she's wearing?"

Drowning in Music

Music flowing into me, I blow a flute, or pipe, I sing a note.
Suddenly I am engulfed in a cloud of music.
Each notelet, perfect in every detail.
Floating within this cloud I become weightless.
Time stands still.
All other thoughts and feelings cease.
Overwhelmed by the wonder of this experience I dive deeper.
I am carried on and on, higher and higher.
Until as quickly as it started, it ends and I am returned back to
earth to reflect in wonder at what had happened
The magic flute.
The flute of magic.
The voice within.
The inner voice.

Dubb Rhythms

The rhythmical reactions,
Are reflected in a reality of realisations.
The turmoil of troubles,
Are tortured by a torrent of toxicity.
The karmic creativity,
Caresses the cares of calamitous collisions.
The echoes of eccentricity,
Excite the ascetic existence.
The inspirational interludes,
Are interrupted by illuminated intervals.
The solemnity of silence,
Seduces the soul into submission.

Evergreens

Some people in our lives are like deciduous leaves they come
in spring budding with new life and energy,
But by autumn they fade and are blown away in the wind.
Others are like the evergreens that stay strong and rich in
colour.
Deep green lasting all seasons, not affected by the changes.
Sometimes we feel bare and friendless like winter trees,
Striped of the canopy of companions.
At others, new relationships burst forth opening up and
unfolding in front of our eyes,
Like the fresh new shoots of spring,
Lush from the barren months of winter.
Yet in those dormant months in our season of isolation we
reflect and build on our inner strength.
Until we are ready to draw up from our roots the knowledge
and power we have gained.
So through all our seasons and with the strength of our,
evergreens to bring us colour and true friendship,
We will stand proudly in the bright sun of summer days
Hold fast to our reserves through the harness of winter chill.
From tender slim sapling to wider girth of age and wisdom
The grace of nature takes its course.

Everybody has to earn a Living Somewhere

Everybody has to earn a living somewhere, I just wish they'd earn it somewhere else.
The phone rings, double glassing, you've won a holiday, can I speak to your husband, we have special offers, your home insurance.

Everybody has to earn a living somewhere, I just wish they'd earn it somewhere else.

The door bell rings, clean your windows, our religion is best, will you vote for me, there are five hundred channels with us, you didn't pay your parking fine.

Everybody has to earn a living somewhere, I just wish they'd earn it somewhere else.

Letter box claps, weekly local rag, circular for the BNP, you've won a million pounds if you just buy The Readers Digest, directionally dyslexic Mini Cabs under new management, Dodgy Antiques will call in your area today.

Everybody has to earn a living somewhere, I just wish they'd earn it somewhere else.

Driving in the car, I'll wash your windscreen, can't park there, did you know your light is not working, only five pounds to wash your car, twenty roses five pounds, any DVD latest films only ten pounds.

Everybody has to earn a living somewhere, I just wish they'd earn it somewhere else.

Trip to the West End, spare some change for some tea, harmonica played out of tune, move down the line there's room at the end of the platform, where is your ticket.

Everybody has to earn a living somewhere, I just wish they'd earn it somewhere else.

Crossing the road, black cab stops by your feet, Royal Mail in a race to the death, motor cycle messenger think he owns the road, juggernaut keeps your breath, police car destroys most of your hearing.

Everybody has to earn a living somewhere, I just wish they'd earn it somewhere else.

Shopping, fresh fruit displayed in the front, yet what you get is picked from a box in the back, a bargain offer with half of it missing, (what's new), the street vendor who shouts in your ear, the cake that looks so delicious but is better left on display, the CD with only one good track on it.

Everybody has to earn a living somewhere, I just wish they'd earn it somewhere else.

An evening in front of the TV, game shows without any meaning, sports programmes that race nowhere, the oldest films ever made, the soap that washes over large issues, reality shows that are far from reality and discussions with nothing to say.

Everybody has to earn a living somewhere, I just wish they'd earn it somewhere else.

Filigree and Shadow

Youth without wisdom and wisdom without youth.
Inspired by words and sound.
A celebration of discovery, the freedom of thought,
Released from caged conformity.
Transcending the restrictions of body and mind,
The spirit flys, the heart is opened.
Filigree and shadow pass across my minds eye
Fever tree reflections of where my destiny may lie.
Songs of distant decades, shadows cast on past lives.
Silken threads of wisdom, on which my history survives.
Gossamer on misted dew, sunsets to moonbeam.
Patents new unbroken, entering the ages decline.
Painted on a dream freeze, woven with the soul tears.
Soft within the songs breeze, voices breath reflections.
Harmony on soul-scape, filigree and shadow.
The journey of experience, echoing my spirit calls.

For Whom The Bells Toll

We open our hearts to tears or to laughter.
We plunder our memories for joy from the past.
Singing the praises of hope filled with wonder.
We walk into doorways into the unknown.

Cruel hands may fate us, but love will prevail.
Solemn forgiveness of what is to come.
Stark realisation on mountains of pain.
Joyful reunion of light's inner peace.

Guided by instinct beyond comprehension.
The choice, it is taken; the deed, it is done.
Ours is our destiny brokered by karma.
In pursuit of truth, measured by time.

Infinite questions, microscopic conclusions.
Awakening consciousness, as the dawning bell tolls.
Eyes now opened, sleep now past.
Journeys now ended where once they begun.

Fortune Tales

Fortune tales of countless battles.
Rebound echoes of silent screams.
Dreams awakened with hardened moonlight.
Passionless eyes in empty space.
Forests of living, fallen, dying.
Walk no more with troubled brow.
Cut down in Spring time.
Buried in Autumn.
A Summer's life.
A Winter's farewell.

From the Spent Embers of the Past

From the spent embers of the past, a flame is kindled,
Igniting light and warmth into the present.
A voice unspoken speaks.
Visions of images unknown are projected into this transient moment
Caught on the wind.
Seen through aged wisdomed eyes.
Memories unshared are loaned.
To catch a glimpse of a movie that is someone's life.
Imaged through the frames of existence.
Moments, seconds, years.
Time lost, now found.
A treasure-trove of unanswered questions.
The volcano of emotions rising, erupting.
Rushing outwards, smouldering tears burn into the soul.
Cascades of molten lava tears spill into consciousness,
Cool and harden to produce new shapes new form, new layers of being.
Releasing forever the caged the captured prisoner of silence.
The depth of contact immeasurable .
An unending well, whose waters quench the parched reserves of barren wasteland,
Whose borders once closed are now opened setting free.
The burned traveller to continue with a lighter load.
A lighter heart.
A cherished heart moment.
That will only be lost by death.

Gift

We pass from life to life, from form to form.
From a flower, to a raindrop.
Each feeding one another on it's journey to feed itself.
Our universal connection within, emanation without.
Clear for those who have the eyes to see.
As a raindrop joins a stream which merges with the ocean,
Then begins its journey once more.
So we from life to life, experience the creation,
Both within and without.
And in doing are both separate and apart of the whole.
The oneness of creation broken apart to enable itself to
experience what it is to be a flower or a raindrop.
Now in our journey, in this human form we learn the real pain
and joy of separation from our true selves.
So our gift, is our ability to unite with creation deep within
ourselves and recognise that experience in the creation that
surrounds us,
From the smallest insect to the passing look of a stranger,
From the beauty of a sunset, to the joy and warm hug of a
child.
The vibration that sustains the universe is held within us,
Resting like the most delicate of all flowers for us to recognise
and then to protect it from the harness of the world.
Our journey homeward is shared with others,
But by our own understanding of ourselves and the recognition
of the truth that lies within.
So we are both student and teacher,
Child and adult,
Creation and part of creation.
Each breath a journey in itself.
A step, one from and one to the beginning.
A circle within a circle,
Lifetimes within a life
Our inner voice, beyond mind and body,
Is our soul's connection to infinity.

GOD

Generator, Operator, Destroyer.

The generator of life energizes our first moments.
Breathing life into our small bodies and showering us with the spark of love.

The operator of life sustains us with the power that sustains the universe.
As we breathe.
As we look.
As we move.
As we touch.
As we grow.
Our consciousness blossoms until.

The destroyer of life gathers us up.
Like the buds of spring through rich green leaves of summer.
The golden brown leaves turn to dust only to regenerate the tree of creation.
Generator.
Operator.
Destroyer.
GOD.

Grief

Each encounter with mortality that happens seems unreal yet
more real than reality itself.
A mist thick and dark is dragged across our consciousness
and the soul weighs heavy with a pain that is both
Inexplicable and unbearable.
Logic and reason vanish.
A spiralling of emotions rise up like a plains twister.
Whirlwinds of memories, events and situations trigger
explosive reactions.
Anger, fear, regrets, loss and pain melt together pulling the
very essence of our being into a torrent of feelings, like a river
as it rushes over the edge of a high waterfall.
Emptiness, a void follows this rush of internal activity.
But what thin veil, what ethereal curtain stands between us
and death
Between us and the ones we love
Knowing that this is our destiny too.
That we will also leave grieving, the living to carry the burden
of life's journey
What is our true purpose, what is our true reality.
Are we graced to have known and loved the ones we lose to
deaths cold touch.
We may cry a thousand tears.
Our hearts break into a thousand pieces.
Our souls tortured by a thousand primordial screams.
But we are alive
And our flesh that houses our soul.
The eyes that we look through.
The ears that we hear with.
And the breathe we breathe,
Is a gift beyond our understanding.
We feel this grief because we are a breathing, feeling being.
Our consciousness knows we are mere mortals.
But our soul lives on and in our actions of love.
We share immortality with those who love us.
Judge and be judged.
See and be seen.
Love and be loved.
Give and receive all of life's gifts.
Death is but a doorway the path we have yet to walk.

Happiness

Happiness is not a commodity that can be frozen or dried,
To be defrosted or re-hydrated,
When our stores of happiness run dry.
You can't trade in happiness,
Buying by the pound or selling by the kilo,
Or look in the store cupboard for a can of condensed
happiness.
Its not found on the preserve shelf in Asda or Sainsbury's.
Happiness is mysterious.
A magical ingredient that makes the meal of our lives.
Taste sweet or spicy, sensational or warming.
Turning a bland stew into a banquette.
It is not found in others yet others have the power,
To open up the happiness inside us.
It can be shared, yet it is a solitary experience.
It is constant yet our understanding of it is transient.
We strive for it and mourn its passing.
It has the innocence of children
And the contentment of age.
It can erupt like a volcano.
Or be safe like a warm blanket on a winter's night.
Happiness is free,
Yet its cost is having the freedom to realise it.
The deeper we dive into our own understanding,
The more constant is our experience.
Through the passing of pain,
We find the value of happiness.
And finding the value of happiness
We pass through the pain.

Heads Up Asses

Chatter, chatter heads up asses, chatter, chatter chattering
classes.
Dissecting art into minuet pieces.
Determining artists as a rare and extinct species.
Reflecting the complexities of their navels.
The truth of creativity tuned to fables.
Chatter, chatter heads up asses, chatter, chatter chattering
classes.
Conformity within structured confines.
Compound interest of credit declines.
Opinions, reactions, based in contempt.
Visionary practitioners, emotions spent.
Chatter, chatter heads up asses, chatter, chatter chattering
classes.
Spirit and soul an unvalued currency.
Experienced originality, successful redundancy.
Form and text within bonded rules.
Numerical equilibrium the recognized tools.
Chatter, chatter heads up asses, chatter, chatter chattering
classes
Standing alone defying convention.
Art within art, a home without pretension.
Soured from within by experience's wheel.
The strength not in thought, but what we feel.
Chatter, chatter heads up asses, chatter, chatter, chattering
classes

I Stand Naked in the Grand Hall of the Mansion of Time

I stand naked in the grand hall of the mansion of time.
My cloak of protection cast off to reveal the reality of my
existence.
Judged by my thoughts and deeds.
My words reflect my realisations and understanding.
I bow my head in shame for the mistakes, unpremeditated and
for the pain projected onto others.
For my unconscious being who tramples on the delicate petals
of others' lives.
I look up with the eyes of a small child.
My innocence no excuse for my deeds of injustice.
As I have done to others so they stack their pain upon my
own.

Here amidst the vast grandeur of infinity I am a small speck of
consciousness.
Struggling to comprehend my own existence in a universe of
changes and wonder.
My soul has been my sanctuary in a world of treachery and
deception.
My pathway to this mansion has disappeared behind me.
Blown away by the wind of truth.

And so I stand naked in the grand hall of the mansion of time.
Respectfully baring my essence to the elements of judgement.
All eyes and yet no eyes are upon me.
For only my inner eye can reveal to myself my true identity.
To stand naked beyond body, flesh and personality.
To rip open all wounds bareing their tenderness and crying.

Here I stand naked in the grand hall of the mansion of time.
I am a witness to the duality of mind and soul.
Of body and spirit, of turmoil and tranquillity, of birth and death
The long journey of our destinies.
Caught in a moment of pure consciousness.

In An Uncertain World

There is no certainty in an uncertain world.
Trains may run on time or they may not.
It might rain tomorrow or it may not.
The people you may think hate you today.
Could tomorrow be the ones who love you.
An opinion you may have held for years and is fixed in stone.
Could suddenly be changed for ever by one phone call.
There is no certainty in an uncertain world.
Our overpowering fears and foibles.
That have plagued us all our lives can be washed away for ever.
The prejudice and ignorance of ourselves and others,
Can be shown for what they are by the death of the past,
Or the birth of the future.
There is no certainty in an uncertain world.
The plans we make may come to nothing,
Or an impulsive, intuitive action can change our lives for ever.
The seeds we plant may not grow,
But others that have lain dormant for years,
Suddenly spring to life.
There is no certainty in an uncertain world.
The people we think are our friends desert us in our darkest hour
And the person we least expect has the strength and vision to carry us through.
When we lose all hope in ourselves and others,
Some small thing can restore our faith and give us the courage to carry on.
There is no certainty in an uncertain world.
Only the certainty of uncertainty.
What seems uncertain at the beginning of the day,
May not be certain by the end.
What may seem unobtainable is attained .
What seems unbelievable becomes a reality.
What is unknown is learnt.
There is no certainty in an uncertain world.
Therefore anything can happen,
If we are certain,
That, that is what we want to happen.

In Fear of the Future

We can only overcome our fear of the future,
By letting go of the past and moving into the present.
The security that the past holds for us, is an illusion so fragile
that the subtlest movement will shatter into a million pieces,
leaving us in a vacuum of unreality, a no man's land of
confusion.
But with our roots planted firmly in the past, we can stand
proudly in the present and greet the future with expectation
and excitement,
To hold out our arms with joy, say goodbye to the past,
Leaving the dead leaves of Autumn to become the fresh buds
of Spring.
To leave behind the journeys of yesterday, to travel into
tomorrow,
Where the unknown becomes a bright new calling.
An awakening call to greet,
A new day,
A new beginning,
A new adventure on life's funfair.

In Lovers' Dreams

In lovers' dreams.
When orchids bloom and passioned flowers grow evermore.
Perfumed moments with fragrant glance, ageless longing,
Sweat embrace.
Enlightened touch, the heart filled wonder.
Karmic encounter.
In lovers' dreams.
In lovers' dreams.
No mountains left, no thoughts unsaid.
Each moment lived, as would be the last.
Honest words from truth lit eyes.
Playful sorrow, hopes eternal, walk in grace
In lovers' dreams.
In lovers' dreams.
The road is endless, parallel in joint refrain.
Voiced in harmony of spirit, searched now ended.
Partnered one, two companions.
Love's cup flowing, kindred souls
In lovers' dreams.
In lovers' dreams.
Each day living, life together.
Understanding what is true.
Dreams become, our ever waking moments
Heritage divine.
In lovers' dreams.
In lovers' dreams .
In lovers' dreams.

In Others

In others as in myself, I see darkness and light.
The struggles, the battles, the wars of inner turmoil.
Faith is a casualty of such skirmishes, hope the wounds,
Peace is a hard, hard fought victory.
One that is never safe.
The borders of our consciousness are forever under attack.
We must never be off guard.
The surrounding moving armies of darkness,
We can see and know only too well.
But a smiling face may hide the cracks in our defences.
Look for the light within ourselves and others,
Creation speaks in many voices and through many forms.
First we must listen, then we can see that the serenity of
A blackbird or a robin can never be questioned.
Yet within ourselves where does our serenity lie?
To keep the faith.
To hope for hope itself.
To strive for inner peace.
Where consciousness abounds.

Our Children

In our children we invest the future of humanity.
Charging them to learn from our mistakes.
As we have learned from the wisdom and follies of generations
that have past before.
They are the part of ourselves that we do not own or cannot
cling to
Yet we nurture and love them, protecting them from the
harshness of the elements.
Guiding them through the maze of life's obstacles and
misfortunes
We watch them laugh and cry sharing both their criticisms and
their praise.
Preparing them and grooming them for their journey.
We stand and stare as they disappear into their own lives.
They are our parents' parents and our children's children.
Becoming the future, yet firmly rooted in the past.
We see the likeness of others and the similarities of our
selves.
The voices of our parents and the actions of their own
children,
They unlock and open a deep-rooted need in us.
To give birth to the future and remorse for deeds undone.
For words unspoken, for the regrets of all that could have been
and hope for all that will follow.
We hold in our hearts the one important and all encompassing
thought,
That no matter what could have been or what will follow,
We love them more than life itself.

In Our Dreams

In our dreams, we visit poppy fields and orchid rooms with
perfumed rays of light walking tiptoe in silent refection.
Our breath ebbs and flows like the sea tickling the shoreline.
Candid mirrors dissolve into landscapes.
Water buffalos and the smiles of children turn tears into
butterflies, delicately visiting the petals of flowers on a warm
summer day.
Waterfalls of memories metamorphose from seagulls to
eagles.
From balconies of affection, to a spider's web of reality.
Friends become entries in journals
Childhood memories transcend time and are relived through
misted tear drops, prisms of elusion.
Danger rides in.
Like the darkness.
On a stallion of destruction, cloaked in the armour of evil.
Brandishing his weapons of hatred and fear.
He enters our consciousness like the wind rushing down a
dark alleyway.
Forcing closed doors open, turning order into chaos.
Disturbed we fight back, returning to the dawn chorus of our
existence.
Chimes of tranquilly, awaken embers.
Beauty hidden deep, treasure chests of understanding and
enlightenment.
Realisations explode like sunburst rainbows through storm
clouds.
Time is stretched and condensed.
The hall of mirrors in funfair reflections.
Images of ourselves that exist only in the dreams of others.

In Praise of Creation

In the church of creation,
The sun is the alter and the wind the hymns of praise.
Earth and water are the sacraments and humanity the priest and priestess.
The universe is the building and the sky the stained glass windows.
Services are infinite and endless and worship a joy.
Nature is the Bible, salvation is all around us.
Peace abounds and beauty is in the eye of the beholder.
In the church of creation.

In the Chambers of My Heart

I walk beyond the boundaries of my consciousness.
I hear the voice of my soul echoing, in the chambers of my heart.
I view visions of a reality in microscopic detail.
Blinded by light I am guided by a strength of purpose,
Directed into unknown un-chartered waters.
My spirit is my pathway and creation's power surrounds me.
Fear and pain have walked beside me on this journey,
Yet they accompany me not.
Doubt has visited me often but leaves without notice.
Hope, I welcome and enjoy its company.
At the end of this long adventure awaits death,
A doorway from one lifetime to another.
On these travels I have died and been re-born many times anew.
I am both student and teacher, child and adult.
Aged with years, I look through my windows that are my eyes,
As would a small child.
My curiosity is boundless.
My understanding becomes less the more realisations unfold.
Like pouring a litre of water into an eggcup.
It flows through me and over me.
Washing my consciousness with creation's love.
I am unworthy of my path.
I wish only to be re-united with creation.
To rest the rest of the weary traveller home at last.

I am an enigma to myself and others.
I carry the stigma of the outsider.
The scars of persecution and ignorance are carved deep into my psyche
The ghosts that haunt me are exorcized by the love that others show me
And I return to them
I am neither male nor female, body or spirit
Duality in unity, Diversity in one.

In The Dream Court

We reinvent ourselves, moment by moment.
In our dreamlike states, or in heightened awareness,
Our beliefs become historical works,
As in dreams we once had despair.
Floodlight curtains open unto our stage for the day.
And the rapturous applause melts into silence.
Lions become sleeping lambs and crabs walk into the mouths
of sharks.
Eagles forget to fly and bury their heads in the sand.
But castles not built to last stand defiant against the ravages of
the sea.
Our unpredictable nature, holds court with tradition.
On trial we plead guilty to the charge
And re-evaluate the consequences of each other's actions.
The scales of injustice, find, guilt by association,
In the knowledge of oneself.

In the Eye of a Storm

In the centre of a storm is a stillness, a calm the remains
unaffected by the turmoil that surrounds it.
This is said to be the eye of the storm.
We have such an eye, a place within, unburdened by the
complexities of worldly existence, self sufficient in its purity
and untouched by the egos of ourselves and others.
A centre point of safety, in the hurricane of life, a true home in
the wilderness of existence, an oasis in the deserts of time.
Our eye that knows and sees all, is our link with the moment.
Our connection with infinity, a meeting point of body, mind and
soul.
The merging of illusion into reality.
Where truth is and where knowledge is known and ignorance
forgotten.
This harbour, or port in a storm, is a jewel that is so precious
that our life is not our life without it.
When we look on its glow, its warmth, we want to bathe
forever in its glory.
To cast off the shadows of yesterday and rush into the future
with every part of our being.
For with this eye, unseen by others, yet mirrored in the eyes of
humanity, we are safe beyond the realms of fear.
We can rest and know a peace that all who seek will be sure to
find.
In the eye of a storm.

The Solitude of Silence

In the solitude of silence, rests a universe of experience,
An all encompassing ecstasy, of peace and understanding.

In the solitude of silence, waits a resting place for the weary,
From life's tiring cavalcade, to the silence of the night.

In the solitude of silence, lies a waterfall of truth,
Washing away misunderstanding and turning darkness into
light.

In the solitude of silence, there is a warmth and understanding,
Measured only by our wiliness, to stop and enter in.

In the solitude of silence, grows the root of all creation,
Captured by a timeless breath, caught by us in silent prayer.

In the solitude of silence, love will lift away all doubts,
And cast away our fears as we journey to our home.

In the solitude of silence, is the path that we must follow,
Of all learning and reality, where light embraces all.

Is Love

Love cannot be bought, love cannot be sold
Can love be commanded, can love be sold?
Is love a substance, is love a form?
Where love is broken, can new love be born?
Would love give happiness, would love give grief?
If love brings happiness, will love bring relief?
Is love a golden ring, is love made of vows?
Is love never parting, is love having rows?
Could love heal bad memories, could love end all sorrow?
If love is here inside my life, will love be here tomorrow?

It's Hard

It's hard to change the patterns of a lifetime,
To turn back the pages of time.
It's hard to release the iron grip of others,
To set free the child within.
It's hard to let the tears flow freely,
To walk on our own pathway.
It's hard to step proudly forward
And grow tall in no one else's shadow.
It's hard to walk in our own shoes
And not follow the road someone else has made.
It's hard to nurture our own vulnerability,
Whilst acknowledging the fears we fear.
It's hard to be who we really are,
When we spend a lifetime being who we are not.
It's hard to let others love us,
When we are unable to love ourselves.
It's hard to ask any new questions,
When we are always told that we are such a fool.
It's hard to laugh with others,
When we are unable to laugh at ourselves.
It's hard to learn new lessons,
When by unlearning our knowledge is complete.
It's hard to know if the creator loves us,
When we are not in love with the creator.

I've kept the company of darkness

I've kept the company of darkness; I've danced with the Devil.
I've stared evil in the eye; I've met it face to face.
It lures you in, soothes you softly like the night.
Making you feel supreme.
Then eats away at your very being and chips away at your heart.
It courts you first with style and promise, as if you are in control.
But as you loosen up your defences, it crushes your very soul.
It comes in many forms and faces, lovers, friends, who knows?
But unaware we let it in then fight the battles old.
We are but children aged with time,
Cursed by this confrontation.
But the light within us will prevail and guide us to our home.
So journey carefully, guard yourself well and protect your hidden treasures.
Know the darkness when it calls and hold your lantern high
For all creation rests within you.
As darkness falls, so light must chase away all shadows.
Be not afraid, fear breads fear, as love will conquer hate.
Just know yourself stand straight and walk into your destiny.

I Watch the Nightingale

I watch the nightingale and hear her song,
I seek salvation,
Yet salvation passes by.
I am a restless spirit,
A searcher, a wanderer.
I look with the eyes of the all knowing,
I feel with the innocence of a child,
I am all, yet nothing.
I am full, yet empty.
The causeway of life's journey rides high and picturesque,
Yet my carriage is broken, my horses are lame.
So I tread the footpaths in hope of sustenance and rest.
I pass through thicket and forest,
Until there, in a clearing,
I watch the nightingale and hear her song.

Just Words

If a whisper is a lie
And a lie becomes a lifetime
Is anger a reflection of the hopelessness inside?
Can the tormented torture others?
Or victims victimise?
Is reality unreal?
Or can the blind see insight?
Are reflections merely mirrors?
Or divisions divided parts?
Can a raindrop make an ocean?
Or a kiss break a heart?
Does love end with hatred?
Or hatred end with love?
Are humans really human?
Or is mankind unkind?
Can we listen with our inner ears?
And see with open eyes?
Can the words we speak reflect the truth that lies deep inside?
Are our thoughts who we are?
Or our deeds who we are not?
Can we be judged by others and judge others not?
If our pain is deep and hurtful
Should we pass it to another?
Or give love instead of hatred?
Give light instead dark?
If you cut me will I bleed?
If you hurt me will I cry?
If you love me will I love you?
If you kill me will I die?

Learn to Play

The subtlety of passion, gives love its own reaction.
Don't turn away, learn to play.
Let life be your director, you are your own creator.
Come from within, time to begin.
Each moment is a new one, so shed the past and move on
Keep riding high, live not die.
Cry aloud your feelings, joy to know its meaning.
Your soul on fire, burns with desire.
As you find your beginning, it sets your body spinning.
Turns dark to light, gives some a fright.
Make your way and make it good, let the whole world come as
it should
The horseman rides, takes all in his stride.
Calling out to you, be strong, be true.
Make happiness, leave unrest.
Race to race, face to face.
The givers and the takers, the users and the makers.
Discretion's song, harmony not wrong.
People of sensations give heart, yet who will start?
It's them not us, don't cause a fuss.
Life in the bins, judged of your sins.
Sentences unfold, no truth yet told.

Life is a Carnival

Life is a carnival coloured by love and hate.
Oceans part, people turn and walk away.
Joy and sorrow pass equally through the gauntlet of eternity.
The sonnets of souls held fast by the motionless balance of
truth.
Clouded skies weep rainbow tears,
Turn icy landscapes into memorised sunsets.
Volcanic emotions erupt, forming new horizons,
Tearing old from new, they forge beauty and grace.
From echoes of past and present future, waits the calling,
Sad goodbyes bring forward the long awaited return.
Justice and hope merge to bring the balance of life and death.
Journeyed strangers pass glancing smiles that are washed
away by doubtful expectations and sombre thoughts.
Innocence restored, the crown of the giving is placed,
As noble spirits unite and join in the oneness of love

Look

When we truly look into the eyes of another,
We see truth looking back at us,
A mirror of our mortality and immortality.

Look and You will Find

There is a beauty beyond all bounds.
All who look are filled with awe.
Perfection found in formless wonder.
Contemplation of total completeness.
No worldly touch to spoil or falter.
Clarity of thought.
Purity of deed.

Moments of Inspiration

At moments of inspiration, when the light of creativity burns
brightly.
Then the stillness of the mind and the passioned experience
hold court with the soul.
There in that moment of all encompassing beauty, when we
surrender our intellect and release the power deep within
ourselves.
We commune with our higher consciousness and have
knowledge of our true selves, undaunted by the opinions or
reactions of others unfettered by the constraints of our
restrictions,
From this place we look out at the world and wonder at its
immense complexity.
Each word we write, each note we sing, each delicate stroke
of the brush,
Desperately trying to describe that feeling, that moment of
sheer bliss.
At moments of inspiration, when the light of creativity burns
bright,
Heaven is just a breath away.

Moon on the Water

Moon on the water, reflections of light and dark
Moon on the water, a liquid reality flowing over solid truth
Moon on the water, the beauty in illusion captured from a
droplet of consciousness
Moon on the water. Feminine gyle in a masculine domain
images of divinity seen through finite eyes
Moon on the water, ebb and flow of tides, cycle of cycles
ripples in a universe, licking the shoreline of our lives
Moon on the water, distance and time merging as one
Moon on the water, spirit of hope, infinitely sublime
Moon on the water, light reflecting wisdom into a prism of souls
Moon on the water, Moon on the water.

Moving Image

I see myself as, images, words and music,
Sculptured out of fiction into fact,
Painted on a canvas of conscious and unconscious realities,
A film in which I write the dialogue, shoot the scenes and edit
rushes.

But in reality I am an extra in a huge production of infinite
proportions,
With a cast of billions, filmed over trillions of years,
Sometimes I wish I could ask the director to edit out some of
the parts,
Frame by frame.

But then my character would not make sense and this is the
director's cut,
Only he has the true screen play in mind, the bigger picture,
I may have grandiose ideas, but in this film,
Every living thing plays lead and supporting roles.

We all play an integral part in the film 'Creation,'
By the director of;
'Ice Age', 'Black Holes,' 'Light' and 'The Big Bang,'
An' Infinite Universe' production!

Nana (My Grandmother)

You remember when cars were in a minority to horse drawn carriages
And brown bread was the cheapest bread to buy.
You remember the first films, Charlie Chaplin and the Music Halls.
You remember planes with four wings and men going off to war after war.
You remember the first recordings, the birth of radio and Art Deco.
You remember electric lights replacing gas lamps, the first telephones and airships across the Atlantic.
You remember coal fires, frosty mornings and long hot summer nights.
The farthing, silver sixpences and large five pound notes.
You remember the rise of Hitler, Mussolini and Stalin's Russia.
You remember the Blitz, the Holocaust, the yanks and Armistice day.
You remember the birth of my mother, her laughter, her tears and her smile.
You remember her childhood, adolescence and her as a young and beautiful woman.
You remember the first television, bananas and oranges after the war.
You remember me as a baby, the walks, my first steps and my smile.
You remember my life, your life and the life of my mother.
You remember a century past, lives lost and saved.
You remember so much and I will always love and remember you.

Nature's Treasured Jewel

The sea shimmers like a treasure chest of darkened gems,
reflecting heavenly
Light.
As the sun misted in clouds, stretches out beams, like fingers
caressing the water's edge.
Rainbows paint spectrums of colour and melt into the velvet
ocean.
Oystercatchers rush and call to each other their song, merging
with the tranquil rhythms of the lapping waves and washing on
the rocks and stones being worn smooth by the turning tides of
many moons.
Seals peep out of their secret world, to investigate and view -
the voyeurs of Nature's feast.
From sunrise to sunset, through rain, storms or sunny days.
A changing yet dependable beauty exists.
Unaffected by progress or time.

Night, Night

Night, night, make sure the bed bugs don't bite,
We tuck up our children, making double sure
We hug and kiss them and love them more.
Night, night, make sure the bed bugs don't bite.

As we read them stories and take them to an imaginary land,
Their eyes fill with wonder, as their minds understand.
Night, night make sure the bed bugs don't bite.

Just one more glass of water, one more story told,
More hugs and kisses, no matter how old.
Night, night make sure the bed bugs don't bite.

Their sleepy eyes closing, heads heavy on the pillow,
Reminiscing the days fun, the river, touching willow.
Night, night, make sure the bed bugs don't bite.

Laughter fades gently away, running comes to rest,
Dancing with the wind, the freedom they know best.
Night, night, make sure the bed bugs don't bite.

These souls, old and new, caught in this tiny form,
Asleep now at last, awake, unaware of the nights storm.
Night, night, make sure the bed bugs don't bite.
Night, night, make sure the bed bugs don't bite.

Night Talk

You speak to me in voices,
Asking questions without answers.
Demanding,
Commanding.
The quiet easy-going person by day
Becomes Bodicea by night,
Joan of Arc fighting for justice,
Connecting threads of consciousness,
Words and sentences stab out,
Like spears being thrust into the enemy.
I wake and join in your sleeping conversation,
You engage me in this nocturnal banter,
Reverberating streams of consciousness,
Poor out.
I am confused,
Then, I remember you are a night talker!
You sleep talk,
Your body sleeps, whilst you talk!
And I converse with your sleeping self.
Sometimes I wonder about my own sanity,
I am talking to someone,
Who is asleep!

Pathway

Through the uncertainty of life,
We weave a pathway of our own making,
Guided by the desire for truth.

Playtime in Life's Garden

We persecute our innocence out of existence,
The child inside us is left homeless,
Without a friend or guardian.
The charred remains of cremated thoughts,
Are blown in the wind.
Exhumed emotions haunt the present,
Like the shrill call of the banshee,
Penetrating every part of our being.
Frozen memories melt,
Like mountain streams falling from the snow,
Of water surging over rocks in an energetic expression,
Of power and force.
The perfumes of childhood permeate,
As we reclaim the heritage of youth,
To see once again the cloud filled skies.
And watch the frosted meadows reflecting jewelled sunlight.
To breathe the fragrance of Nature's communion,
The return of innocence,
Playtime in life's garden.

Questions

What is the colour of love?
What is the price of freedom?
If there is safety in numbers, where do you stand alone?
Is there hope in tomorrow or pain in yesterday?
Can a kiss wash away sorrows or should demons be faced?
If we look in the mirror do we see ourselves, or just a
reflection?
Can a lifetime be over in a breath,
Or by taking one step towards the truth, caste off the shroud of
illusion?
Is there really a sweet smell of success and putrefaction in
death?
Is revenge mine, or should the balance be held in the hands of
something greater than our emotions?
Is our strength our ability to know ourselves and are there
really so many questions?
If so, why?
Are we responsible for our actions, or are our actions
responsible for who we are?
Is time the great healer, will we heal in time?
Who is the questioner, do we expect an answer?
All these questions, still we ask why?
Yet we know all the answers, at some deeper level we all
know,
Why?

Rebuilding

Sometimes we airbrush out our memories.
The harsher realities of our timewarn existence.
Or mistakes best forgotten, or lessons unlearned.
The jagged landscape smoothed away with each soothing mist of spray.
Leaving fairy tale childhood, to dance into a perfectly formed adult nirvana.
But paint, no matter how expertly skilled the practitioner, will tarnish, fade and peel.
Cracks appear in our idyll, portraits of bygone decades or moments caught in perfumed taste.
Then the real work begins, rebuilding our lives.
From foundations to ridge.
Brick by brick.
Roof truss to facia.
Cleaning away the rubble.
Leaving room for today's landscape,
To be free from the debris of the past.

Relations

We have a relationship with our relations,
Not one we chose, but one chosen for us.
Maybe by fate, or perhaps some genetic gene.
We love our lovers,
Keep the company of our companions.
And befriend our friends
Sometimes we try to forgive our parents,
Even love our children,
But relating to our relatives well?
We reminisce about our distant cousins,
Who used to visit us as small children.
And recall the agonizing excursions to Great Aunt Elsie's or
awful Uncle Arthur's,
Sitting still for hours not speaking or daring to move unless
one of the superior adults consents to talk to us.
The beautiful large gardens which should have been filled with
adventure had to be approached with delicate respect almost
a funereal piety reserved for memorial gardens,
Not real gardens.
Our grandparents who are thought to come from the dark
ages,
Somehow understand us.
And we in return relate to them in later years.
Our brothers and sisters seem like foreign visitors in our
company as we are in theirs.
But relating to relatives is our duty, or is it?

Responsibility

Were does our responsibility start and finish.
We are responsible for our own actions and deeds but what of thought?
We are responsible for our children, our pets.
But our children grow up, they come of age,
But still we feel responsible.
They may appear to have an adult form, but somehow they remain children.
We of course are not children, we become adults and are obviously adult.
We then decide we must be responsible for our parents, younger brothers and sisters.
We have our children who remain in our eyes children.
We, from the age of eighteen, we are adult.
They can be thirty, forty and fifty and are still children.
Our parents we see as older children.
So when do we become older children?
At what age do we revert from adult back to child?
Of course this is not real,
We all remain children and adult,
Allowing our inner child to play only with people we feel safe enough, secure enough, to allow our inner child to come through,
Some people, sadly, never feel safe enough and lead a life of responsibility, restrictiveness.
But I for one enjoy my inner child, the inner child of others, my children and their children.
So now it's time to play.

Returning

We wash away the dirt of the day and bathe in our hopes of tomorrow.
Cleaning off the grime of our selves and others, we perfume our beings with the love of others.
Basking in their kindness and light, we dry our dampened spirit with the warm embrace of our beloved companion.
Clothed in the silken touch of their caress, we rest our bodies in the safety of their love.
Cleansed by their gaze, we join our love as one, in the sharing of a kiss,
Or the long passion of erotic bliss.
When spirit becomes flesh and flesh becomes spirit.

Rhythms of Africa

I've seen the faces, I've heard the voices,
I've felt the rhythms, of Africa.

I've heard her calling, I've listened clearly,
I've watched with wonder, that is Africa.

I know the crying, the tears of torture,
Passed down by my fathers, to Africa.

But I see the beauty and hear the laughter,
As I shed my tears, for Africa.

She is a princess, a Queen of glory,
Rich beyond richness, Africa.

Imprisoned by standards, laid down by the unworthy,.
Caught in a vacuum, Mother Africa.

Yet she has more treasures, more wealth of truth and wisdom,
Than all her oppressors, Africa.

A continent divided, made small by divisions,
United in its cause, to free Africa.

She will rise like a giant, standing proud and strong,
For the world to recognise, the real Africa.

Casting off all her shackles, breaking free from oppression,
She will move with the grace, that is Africa.

For all who have met her, have fallen for her beauty,
Are overwhelmed by her wisdom and love Africa

She touches your soul and opens your heart,
As she frees your mind, you know Africa.

I've seen the faces, I've heard the voices,
I've felt the rhythms, of Africa.

Sailing

We pass one another like ghost ships in the night,
Looking through the sails and rigging as if they are not there.
Yet we are not alone in the grand consciousness of life.
The oceans, the seas, the rivers that make up our journey.
We crave the company of souls, to see the light on board
another vessel,
Signs of life on the wide expanses of nothingness.
We can look in awe at this vast universe and are guided by the
stars,
But our compass is within us to steer us homewards avoiding
the rough seas, the jagged rocks and dark serpents of the
deep.
We can drift endlessly alone, or we can set sail with others and
feel the safety of the company of soulful sailors on the sea of
consciousness,
That is our life.

Sculptured

The patterns of a life are carved into the time aged timber of
memory,
Deep cut with acute perception,
Delicate unbroken lines of purposeful sensitivity.
Dreamlike images, emerging into simple clusters,
Intricate webs linking past and present.
Totally formed into one subtle sculptured being,
Fashioned with the art of the creator's hand.
The journeyman's skills lent to a transient being,
Conceived from light, travelled through darkness,
Emerging into light once more.
The clarity of each chiselled part realised only in the moment
of its existence.
Observed from different sides, the appearance changes like
passing clouds,
Tantalising the viewer to look deeper.
This work of art that is our lifetime can be observed or left to
build on,
New layers hewn and skilfully created as we pass from day to
day,
Decade into decade,
The heart of an oak,
The spirit of a life.

Sleep

Sleep where we rest from the turmoil of tedium,
Or feast our bodies in soothing solace,
Away from the fatigue of fellowship,
Flying high over scenes unset,
Or diving deeply into un-chartered consciousness,
Visiting childhood nightmares,
Or floating on feathered pillow like clouds,
Meeting strangers and friends alike.
Climbing snow capped mountains
And swimming in crystal su -drenched oceans,
Black and white or technicolor, wide screen or miniature,
The landscape of sleep opens up before us,
As our body lays in wait for the dawn,
We dance a thousand dances on moonbeams,
Riding the shooting stars into tomorrow's dreams,
Breathtaking journeys of uncertainty,
Awakened by the call of today,
Sleep's hand is lifted.

Songs of the Universe

Sing the songs of the universe, beat out the rhythm of time.
Play the melody of life, harmonize with creation's choir.
Listen to the inner music, a composition of our destiny.
An arrangement complex and unique, a symphony sublime.
With the orchestra of humanity, conducted by the hand of creation.
Each movement, each bar, a tonal myriad.
Each note the first and the last, a sonnet set to music.
A journey of blissful sound, interaction of soulful exchange.
Communion with spirit and mind, noted with vivacious divinity.
Cordially divine, celestial in its simplicity.
Sing the songs of the universe, beat out the rhythm of time.

Sonnet for Spring

A Springtime sonnet of horseshoe memories,
Golden leaf now turned to green.
A bluebell carpet with songbird melodies,
Perfumed day breaks, now Winter has gone.

Life beginning from dormant sleepers,
Bursting outwards from inner rest.
Warm from chilled winds' blossomed reminders,
Of Summer horizons on longer days born.

Coats of crisp frost with blankets of snow,
Gone into storage where memories lie.
Green from the grey-time, warm from the cold,
Day from the night as light conquers dark.

A promise now kept,long wait rewarded,
Visitors gone as new ones arrive.
Awake is the squirrel the dormouse, the bee,
Gone are the storm clouds now Springtime is here.

Sound

In every sound we hear, there is a myriad of sounds,
Moving ever out, subtle and more complex than the next.
A bird song on a frosty morning,
A cricket on the plains of Africa.
The dynamics of creation, diverse and wonderful.
Harmonics in harmony with themselves.
As a leaf falls in the wind, rusting its way through the cycle of,
Birth, death and re-birth.
The subtle of sound is as sweet as the orchestrated rhythms of
a stream bubbling over rocks, in haste to journey forward.
We fill our lives with sound, but in the rare moments of still-
ness, when nature's voices sing the chorus of the universe and
our mind stops it's chattering.
Then in that moment we can really see, touch, taste, know and
hear,
The sound of life.

Sovereignty

Who has the sovereignty over our feelings?
Who rules the kingdom that is our inner being?
Where are the borders of our existence?
What is the protocol when one person enters into the territory
of others?
Or others enter into ours?

Stepping Nearer to Truth

I journey through life, in search of truth.
Stopping only at crossroads to determine my way.
Each step I have taken, is a step of deep learning.
Each breath I have taken, is my breath of life.
Troubles have confronted my journeys progress.
I have climbed mountains of despair and viewed the valley of good fortune.
Company has walked with me on this journey.
Some gone ahead and some left behind.
But truth, my goal, always in sight.
Visions of beauty in others driving me forward in my quest.
Motivated by desire and passion for a higher reality.
A reality unreal but real, on this journey without beginning or end.
I turn the pages of the book, finish each chapter with more understanding.
Yet knowing that the further I go, the longer is my journey.
My quest only completed as my breath and I cast of this mortal coil.
To journey home once more.

Storm

As the storm clouds of the past fade into the distance,
Rain soaked memories dry in the warmth of today's sunlight.
I reflect on thundered nights and lightning dawns,
Awakening in a hurricane of chaos.
Floods of tears drowning my every waking moment,
Tidal waves of sadness washing over me.
I have struggled with my own existence,
Taking shelter where I could.
The storm always close by,
These shipwrecked thoughts are part of who I am.
But not the whole picture,
For after all storms there is stillness,
A time of reflection,
This, then, is mine.

Superiority

Looking downwards across the nose,
Offering platitudes of patronising praise,
The sentiments of superiority,
A lifetime of creativity erase.

Sweet Song for a Swallow

Freedom's wings flying over imposing landscapes,
Sweet song for a swallow.
Speed and agility, acrobatic beauty,
Sweet song for a swallow.
Intercontinental reality, movement with the wind,
Sweet song for a swallow.
Nature intuitive, intuitive nature,
Sweet song for a swallow.
Wings in sunset, nurturing young,
Sweet song for a swallow.
Symbols of Summer, from Autumn's departure,
Sweet song for a swallow.
Sea and land, roof top or savannah,
Sweet song for a swallow.
Cycles of birth and death, seasons and time,
Sweet song for a swallow,
Sweet song for a swallow,
Sweet song for a swallow.

Temples of Divinity

The sea is the heartbeat of the world and the rivers and
streams the arteries and veins.
The land is the body and the trees are the lungs.
The result is the same - if we abuse our body or we abuse the
world.
Both are temples of divinity, that can be torn down by reckless
abuse.

The Battle

Through the far off dust clouds, I see them coming.
The darkness was falling, the power they had could be felt even from this distance.
The force they projected was frightening.
This, then is the final battle, I am a small child, they are the dark and evil power that lays in wait, ready to rise up in all men, perhaps in all mankind.
The uncontrolled anger, the uncontrolled lust, the uncontrolled power.
Their strength, their weakness, my weakness, my strength.
I turn to my leader, a good man, pure in spirit.
'What should I do?' I ask. 'You will know'. he replies.
I hide, fear engulfing me, like a mist on a river at twilight.
They are upon us.
Chaos.
Swords meet swords, flesh meets flesh.
Passions and anger rises.
One of them rides towards me, he looks down at me and pierces my very soul with his penetrating glance.
I scream, pain, fear, anger, guilt.
I should resist. I should turn away.
When I look back, I see him falling a smile on his face, a lance through his heart.
Confusion, noise, blood, people running, screaming.
I am alone, the battle continues.
Then the daylight forces the darkness away.
I see women, proud and beautiful, empowered women.
They seem to be healing the sick and wounded.
The dark powers have fled.
I ask, 'Can I trust you?'
One turns and smiles.
I am unsure, where was my mother?
Where had my trust gone?
I see another child, she is alone, afraid unsure.
We look, join hands and run, we are free.
She smiles and I smile.

Her smile is deep, her laughter real.
The battle is far behind us.
We do not look back but enjoy the warm sun on our faces.
The sea is calling,
The future beckons and the past fades away.
As we sit on a rock holding each other tightly and watch the beautiful sunset, the fragrance of the fresh breeze from the sea.
We leave the world behind us.

The Bloodstained Inheritance of an Empire

Where is the inheritance of an empire?
Built on the hypocrisy of the Bible and gun.
Of values enforced by hatred and fear,
By men whose culture,
Values the machine before the creator,
Who can only worship in buildings of brick and stone
And where people are valued by the colour of their skin
And exploitation is not considered a sin.
Where to care for others is considered a weakness
And to ask for freedom is considered a sin.
Where is the inheritance of an empire?
Who would rape a continent
And then take every scrap of paper,
As they close the door.
To divide as they conquer
And pillage as they go.
To use its people,
As they would suck the last drop of orange dry
And cast it unwanted to the earth.
To take its treasures and claim them for themselves,
To plunder its riches and steal its wealth?
This then is the legacy,
The bloodstained inheritance of an empire.

The Burdened Traveller

From the spent embers of the past a flame is kindled,
Igniting light and warmth into the present.
A voice unspoken,
Visions of images unknown are projected into this transient
moment,
Caught on the wind.
Wisdomed eyes,
Memories unshared are loaned to catch a glimpse of a movie
that is someone's life, imagined through frames of existence,
Moments, seconds, years,
Time lost, now found,
A treasure trove of unanswered questions.
Time volcano of emotions rushing outwards,
Smouldering tears burn into the soul,
Cascades of molten-lava feelings,
Spill into consciousness, cool and harden,
To produce new shapes new forms, new layers of being,
Releasing forever the caged bird,
The captured prisoner of silence,
The depth of contact immeasurable.
An unending well whose waters quench the parched barren
wastelands,
Whose borders, once closed, are now opened
For the burdened traveller to continue with a lighter load
A lighter heart,
A cherished moment,
That will only be lost by death.

The Cannabis Man

The cannabis man takes all he can from his day to day existence.
'Cool it man' he says as he takes a long toke from his early morning spliff
'Tomorrow is another day, just chill, have a blow, just relax, don't stress, have a blow, munchies coming on'.
The cannabis man listens to the sounds and watches the world go by.
'Yeh I'm really living life to the full, keeping moving on, excitement,
Well just being is enough, hey have another blow, just chill, to-morrow is another day,
Mao Tse Tung, Das Capital, dreaming of better times,
Stay cool man, the revolution is at hand, still tomorrow is an-other day,
Just roll another spliff and have a break, don't want to wear myself out,
I've got three videos to watch, chill man, tomorrow is another day,
Wow it's dark already, lets roll another and hey, just chill, to-morrow is another day'.

The Child Within

Within us our child waits for the moment of security.
When in the company of those we feel safe with,
We can laugh and play.
Or cry to be comforted.
In the harsh world of strangers, we wear our protective
overcoats to keep out the coldness of others
And stop the frosty glare and icy piercing comments penetrating our defences.
We communicate through plate glass panels and keep our
hearts in the bomb-proof sanctuary of our life's experience.
The lessons of combat on any plain, physical, emotional or
spiritual are hard fought and the wounds are deep and painful.
So we travel in time and space aware of others but contained
within our capsule of isolation.
We long for the company of those we truly trust.
Where layer after layer is pealed away and we can run naked
in the sunlight of their love and be a free child of nature.
A free spirit of love.

The Circle is Complete

With you I've found the love I have searched for.
In your eyes I see the love that I feel.
From your touch is all of love's expression
The words you speak carry your message of love.

Whispers in the mists of time, perfume from a flower,
Skylarks over meadows green, church bells on the hour.
An ankle, knee, an arm, a look, a word that makes a rhyme
A sentence deep in thoughtfulness,
Whispers in the mists of time.

In your perfumed presence hangs the fragrance of love.
As you hear my thoughts your face radiates true love.
As I kiss your lips I feel the power of love exploding,
As our love is one the universe explodes.

Whispers in the mists of time perfume from a flower,
Skylarks over meadows green church bells on the hour.
An ankle, knee, an arm, a look, a word that makes a rhyme,
A sentence deep in thoughtfulness,
Whispers in the mists of time, whispers in the mists of time.

The Creator's Call

The creator's love may touch us all,
The creator's hand may guide us,
The creator's eyes may see our journey,
The creator's light may illuminate the way,
The creator's power may sustain us.
But we must be open to receive the love,
We must be prepared to make the journey,
We must have the eyes to see the way
And we must live our lives.
Because the creator cannot do these things for us,
These are ours and ours alone,
To listen for the creator's call.

The Dawning of a New Day

As the heavy blanket of night is slowly lifted and gentle fingers
of sunlight stretch across the room.
The sleepy quiet is disturbed by the soft sound of raindrops on
a window pain.
Birds welcome a new day with a harmonic chorus of complex
notations,
A fox is heard to call out to its young,
As a dog disturbed by alien sounds sends a warning to be in-
truders,
Cats scamper over fences, returning home in search of food
and rest,
All-night party goers talk in noisy whispers and laugh in
restrained bursts of mirth as they remember the pleasures of
the small hours.
The milk float creaks its slow electric way down small streets,
The smell of fresh cut lawns drift upwards,
Tides change,
Warmth returns,
Perfumed flowers slowly open,
Daylight is upon us,
Shadows are cast-off like winter coats no longer needed, now
Spring has finely arrived,
The subtle interwoven sounds of the night are replaced by the
bustling noises of daytime routines,
All fears that seemed so overwhelming as we began our
nocturnal journey shrink and take on new dimensions,
Like entering and leaving a tunnel,
The darkness before us opening up from a small dot in the
distance, then bursting into light.
So the night passes,
Leaving behind its subtle hidden beauty.

The Last Doorway

As the sun rises in the East and sets in the West,
Death, the final leveller awaits us all,
Kings and queens alike,
Sage and simpleton,
Walk through one last doorway.

The Plumber from Plumstead Common

The plumber from Plumstead Common, earns a very large
amount,
He will come and turn off your stop valve and drain your bank
account.
He drives a new Mercedes and drinks Châteauneuf du Pape,
He sometimes eats quails eggs and listens to Hip Hop and
Rap.

He is very well educated, owns a house in the Algarve,
He's terribly nice and polite, sophisticated and awfully suave.
He only works in the winter, in the summer he goes on retreat,
He is lactose intolerant you know and doesn't eat fish or meat.

He learnt his trade from his father, who lives in a Peckham flat,
He drives an old Morris van and wears a dirty flat hat,
His father would never vote Tory nor Liberal Democrat too,
'I am Labour and always will be, a Conservative that will never
do'.

The plumber from Plumstead Common, reads the Times and
does the crossword.
When asked if he's expensive, 'expensive that's quite absurd.
Quality doesn't come cheap you know, for Bollinger you have
to pay,
If you'd rather drink Asti Spamanti, then hey that's okay.

I am a plumber who gets the job done, burst pipes boilers as
well,
The cheaper the price of the plumber, he's probably the
plumber from hell'.
The plumber from Plumstead Common, is thinking of retiring
next year,
Well I have earned enough in my lifetime and I am thirty-five
my dear.

The Postman and the Poltergeist

The postman and the poltergeist, walked their postal route,
The poltergeist asked the postman if he'd smoke a nice cheroot.
The postman reflected deeply and said 'I think not!'
The poltergeist then asked if he'd like a nice shallot.
'I have neither taste nor inclination for leaf or onion alike!'
So the poltergeist asked the postman if he'd rather ride a bike.
'I walk along my postal route to keep my health each day.
Your chattering does annoy me I wish you'd fade away!'
The poltergeist then pondered on the complexity of a shallot.
If a bike or cheroot will not satisfy,
Then I will try this garrotte,
The postman and poltergeist now walk their ghostly route.
The poltergeist said 'At last I've found something that you suit!'.

The Price of Wisdom

Wisdom cannot be bought or sold.
Each reality peels away a layer of illusion revealing a wider
vision, a deeper understanding
Tears wash away the past and laughter refreshes the present,
As the future stands before us unread, uncharted.
Years pass, we see our children become parents and our
parents become old.
Our grandchildren play as our children have played before,
From grandmother to great grand daughter.
From the wisdom of ages, to the innocence of new beginnings,
Walking along pathways well trodden and pathways unknown,
We share in each others wisdom and understanding,
Learning from one another, wishing only for love to pass from
generation to generation.
For in our own search for truth, wisdom is revealed from all
directions.
So by having the humility to listen to others deeply and read
between the lines,
We gain from them and increase our knowledge,
The only cost is our time, our patience,
Because wisdom cannot be bought or sold and truth is not just
the absence of lies.

THE SATIRIST WHO ONCE WAS KING

The satirist who once was king, held court in a field of wheat,
His voice was loud, the words he spoke,
Brought tears to those he'd meet
And all could hear,both far and near,
The sound that filled the air.
For as they stood, with head to head,
They listened, ear to ear.

You loaves of bread, that soon shall be
Prepared,with yeast and time, listen hard to what I say
And take heed of this rhyme,
Your role in life is clear to see,
From beginning until the end,
To fill men's stomachs,
With a wholesome fare, on this they do depend.

There is much talk of barley grain and stories told of beet,
But the only thing I can be sure, is this simple grain of wheat,
There may be those with corn or oats and rye bread every
morning,
But to pass a day without the wheat, I must now give this
warning.

I've travelled across the widest sea and walked a pretty mile,
I've seen the wonders of the world, but none could make me
smile,
Now I've returned and settled here and watched you grow
from seed
The sun it shone, the rain did fall and there fulfilled your need.

A flower may have a perfume bold and bees may make us
honey
But I see you, beyond all wealth, of diamonds, gold or money,
So stand here proudly, be what you are,
And know this mysterious feat,
Let all that see you recognize,
This golden field of wheat.

The Sea of Troubles

I walk upon a sea of troubles,
No resting place,
No journeys end.
And there amidst the waves of pain,
A voice called out,
Help! Help!
Yet I, so occupied to save myself,
Have turned away,
Have left him there.
But once again the voice did cry,
Help! Help!
I quickened on my journey's way,
Pretending that the wind had called,
But louder now the voice did call.
I turned and moved to meet the sound
And there a boatman,
Called out to me,
He helped me in.
Then softly spoke the boatman's voice,
'The help I called was not for me,
But you!'.

The Struggles of a Lifetime

The struggles of a lifetime can end in a breath.
The breath of a lifetime can end in a struggle.
But with each breath remembered, a life is fulfilled.

The Worth of Words

Know who you are and where you are going.
Know your own worth without the need for the approval of
others.
Do not let the prejudice and conditioning of others distract you
from your chosen path.
Make allowances for others' behaviour to you,
But do not allow them to destroy your confidence or belief in
your self.
You will make mistakes look on them as lessons,
The holes will always be there,
It is up to us whether we fall in them.
Trust in your true self, instinct before intellect.
Do not cloud your judgment with outside or inside stimulation.
Let the lantern of your soul guide you through the fog of life.
Serve the Creator and Creation and allow the Creator and
Creation to serve you.
Be free like the wind but have your feet solidly on the ground.
Wash away the sorrows of yesterday and bask in the bright
sunlight of tomorrow.
Look for positive where there is negative and draw on the
forces of nature to protect you.
Listen with your inner ear, an ant walking, a leaf floating in the
breeze,
The song of life is rich and diverse; music is eternal, ethereal
and everywhere.
Taste your own success and share the nectar of time.
There is joy in giving be bold enough to receive.
Know your own wisdom and listen to the wisdom of others.
Humility does not mean we disrespect ourselves.
Keep a pure heart, an open mind and a thirst for knowledge
and truth will seek you out.

Through the Sunset of Songs

Through the sunset of songs, we hear the voices of distant memories.
The raindrops of tears, that fall upon past oceans of experiences.
Becalmed from the storms of ages form the storms of ages.
Misted by their passing, nebulous like the clouds from the source.
From the small streams beginning, the river has journeyed onwards, passing many banks on its way towards the sea.
The rainbow days of summer, the darkened nights now gone.
Echoed on the winds, the sonnets of the past licking the shoreline of the present.
The waves once fierce and awesome roll backwards into non existence and merge where they began.
Through the sunsets of songs, we hear the voices of distant memories.
The raindrops of tears, that fall upon the past.

Tick Tock

Tick, tock, tick, tock,
The clock is ticking time has passed,
A moment of vision cannot be surpassed,
Tick, tock, tick tock,
Clockwork reflections, digital view,
Pendulum actions each day renew,
Tick, tock, tick, tock,
Solitary moments caught in time,
Visionary actions, feelings sublime,
Tick, tock, tick, tock,
Clock faced smiles, alarmed early calls,
Dawned awakening, sunset falls,
Tick, tock, tick, tock,
Seconds on seconds, hour on hour,
Decade to decade, the movement of power,
Tick, tock, tick, tock,
Light to dusk, darkness to dawn,
Revolving moments as each breath is drawn,
Tick, tock, tick tock,
Time passing slowly, time rushing on,
Time paced steady, time is gone,
Tick, tock, tick tock,
The hour a reminder, the minute a cue,
The second, an inspiration the moment time is due,
Tick, tock, tick, tock, tick, tock, tick, tock,

To be English

From the rhetoric of truths, untrue, to the spin of pub-
philosophers casting its net wide,
The focus group campaigns for the rights of free speech
Paedophilia may be an abomination and cannabis a crime,
Cheaper clothes from abroad well - not in my backyard!
Religion has its place, as do women and children.
We like curry or Chinese meals but Bollywood or the thoughts
of Chairman Mow?
Football is a way of life, a code to live by, in the net,
Kick him, are you blind ref, come on you blues.
What are you looking at?
Of course I don't mean you, you are alright it's the illegals,
Well I'd never let my daughter marry one would you?
Yes I love my country, home of the free, slavery, the holocaust,
3rd world, modern day imperialism, multi-culturalism?
No not round here mate!

What I like is a nice English lager
A glass of scotch or vodka
And down to the Indian for a red hot tandoori or a nice kebab
None of that foreign muck,
That's what being English is all about,
That reminds me, I must take the kids to McDonalds,
My Toyota, no it's great -
No I don't know the words mate
But I will be there for Abba night, they are the best,
Lets have cup of English Tea - good old England!

Tomorrow

Tomorrow I may live or die, tomorrow, tomorrow.
Tomorrow I may sing or cry, tomorrow, tomorrow.
What words I Speak, what truths I seek, tomorrow, tomorrow.

Tomorrow I may understand, tomorrow, tomorrow.
Tomorrow may be new things planned, tomorrow, tomorrow.
What words I speak, what truths I seek,
Tomorrow, tomorrow.

Tomorrow is another day, tomorrow, tomorrow.
But first this one must fade away, tomorrow, tomorrow.
What words I speak, what truths I seek,
Tomorrow, tomorrow.

Tomorrow may be filled with joy, tomorrow, tomorrow.
Tomorrow all my hopes employ, tomorrow, tomorrow.
What words I speak, what truths I seek,
Tomorrow, tomorrow.

Tomorrow the sun will rise anew, tomorrow, tomorrow.
Tomorrow truths may not be true, tomorrow, tomorrow.
What words I speak, what truths I seek,
Tomorrow, tomorrow.

Tomorrow will become today, tomorrow, tomorrow.
But tomorrow I may stay away, tomorrow, tomorrow.
What words I speak, what truths I seek,
Tomorrow, tomorrow,
Tomorrow, tomorrow,
Tomorrow, tomorrow.

Tomorrow Part 2

Tomorrow I will watch the spring flowers opening
And see the frost turn to droplets on the new formed buds of willow,
Tomorrow I will listen as the cuckoos call, as the dawn chorus strikes up like a choir of divinity.
Tomorrow I will welcome the return of the swallows and breathe deeply the perfume of honeysuckle and stocks.
Tomorrow I will bask in the sun's warming rays, eat strawberries and cherries
And contemplate the complexities of time.
Tomorrow I will watch the geese fly noisily away and wonder at the tapestry of golden brown leaves.
Tomorrow I will digest the darkened mornings and the light and shade as the sun hangs low in the sky.
Tomorrow I will run through snow crunching under foot and stand in awe at creation.
Tomorrow I will ask questions, look for answers, love, be loved, laugh, cry, explore my inner self and give thanks.
But tomorrow may never come,
Tomorrow I will?

True Value

We value our actions by the price others put on them,
Not by the true value beyond money or established
recognition.
In our thoughts we project the actions yet to come
And in our deep subconscious self we prepare for the thoughts
that will turn into actions.
Who can say that the gift we give or the action we make has
more value than that of others?
Is money the true value, or that what we do touches the hearts
of others?
Who is richer the merchant or the poet
The singer of songs, or driver of fast cars?
Do we know or even care?
But with a single rose we can open a heart, mend a hurt, and
touch the deepest part of someone's being.
So by our words, thoughts and deeds let us be judged,
Not by the bulges in our purses, wallet or bank account.
For in truth we give all, to all who would hear us
And listen for the truth in others.
Then by our action know the true value of others and
ourselves.

VOID

We, who are born,
Live in fear of death,
Knowing nothing of life,
Are searching for truth,
In a world filled with lies.

Voyage

Sometimes I reflect on the decades of time left in the wake of
my life.
The waves of my actions buffeting the shoreline of the present,
The ripples of feelings and emotion licking the edges of my
being.
As the sunlight of experience enlightens the changes of tides
And the driftwood of friends and lovers float by,
I recall images of childhood rivers flowing into adulterant
estuaries and onto adult seascapes.
Waves from the storms and tempest that I have encountered
Loom up large and fierce
Like a great white shark with mouth wide open ready to
consume me.
But then the reality returns to the ebb and flow of today.
Blown by kind winds I navigate by my inner compass
And steer my worldly vessel clear from the rocks,
Where in times past I have floundered before.
Sometimes buffeted by the passing of another vessel
Or having skirmishes with pirates in search of my soul,
The voyage continues.
Open sea ahead I chart a course and set sail into the future
One day I will dock in the port of death,
Having made the crossing over the sea of life,
Leaving behind the monsters of the deep,
I will prepare for my next voyage,
In the search for the hidden treasure,
Of truth.

Washing over Me

As I journey down the endless universe of my sub conscious,
Images pass and fade into nebulous obscurity.
Words burst into heightened illuminated meaning,
Like new shoots pushing their way into the atmosphere in
search of light.
The osmosis of creativity rises, feeding an inner need.
Sentences are formed from a single word, a seed, lying dormant, underground, waiting for it's moment to burst into flower.
Unaware of time, but in tune with nature.
So as buds open, revealing new growth, I must open myself in
search of growth and awareness.
Setting free my thoughts and releasing my passion.
Allowing the unseen hand to guide my pen, the calm and quiet
inner voice to whisper its reflective remembrances of deep felt
thoughts and subtle imagery.
To release my own limitations and set free the prisoner who
hides within.
The agonies that were once bricked up to keep out the world,
wake to walk in the sunlight drawing in deeply, the breath of
life, allowing the waterfall of the creators love to wash over me
and share that love with others.

Where?

Where are the flags of freedom no longer flying over head?
Where are the songs of victory left floating in the wind?
Where are the doves of peace flown never to return?
Where are the young who died for a cause they did not understand?
Where are the politicians who decided war was the only option?
Where are the innocent victims, collateral damage of destruction?
Where is the new world order demanding equality for all?
Where is the world no longer at war yet peace has not been found?
Where will the United Nations find a way forward?
Where is all the hope that no more blood will be shed?
Where are the lessons of history learned that hate will lead to hate?
Where are the voices who cry out in vain when deathly silence is all that remains?
Where, where, where?

When

When memories are hard and smooth and stories told
un-listened,
When paradise is on the wind and stars that shine
un-glistened.
When roads once walked now lead nowhere and crimson
tears suspended,
Sorrow's fields harvest laughter's kiss all balances are
defended.
When visioned thoughts are left underdone and passioned
dreams un-ended,
Rollercoaster fantasies and wounded hearts un-mended.
When anger left to simmer long becomes its own existence,
Extends its reach to all close by, the line of least resistance.
When scars have healed and new scars form, yet wounds are
left within,
The truth finds ways to free itself and harmony begin.
When freedom's roam is long and hard, with sacrifice at each
turning,
Wisdom's gate it opens out and morning's song left yearning.

Where Consciousness is

Beyond the land of sleep and dreams,
Where battles lost and won are left behind,
Exists a consciousness, illuminated by the light of a thousand
suns,
Where visions of clarity blind the inner eye
And waves of the purest love wash over the parched soul of
suffering.
The sensitive nature of silence is broken down into a myriad of
small details of subtle sound.
The food of life is freely given
And passions taste, is loves refreshment.
Heightened awareness rushes upwards
And freedom's comfort releases the weary and war torn
traveller.
Shackles of illusion drop away,
Unlocked by the key of pure truth.
Knowledge is power,
So knowledge of self is power indeed,
Beyond the land of sleep and dreams,
Where consciousness is.

Where Does

Where does the source of love that I feel for you come from?
How can I measure the volume of emotions that rushes over
me when I hold you?
I've seen great waterfalls in Africa and on islands in Scotland,
But though these torrents of water plummet downwards with
the power of love that I feel for you.
The surge of joy that erupts, like a volcano, with every
intense heat of the sun forcing it's way from the centre of the
planet and from the centre of our being.
This love is physical, but it has its roots firmly in my spiritual
being.
For the love I feel for you comes from my soul.
As I look into your eyes and connect with your essence my
heart bursts into flame.
The light of all creation connects us together, binding our souls
in a karmic link of love.
The rings we wear, symbols of the bond we feel.
The passion you arouse.
The joy you make me feel.
And how safe I am in your arms
No symbols or words can ever describe,
No analogies or graphic description can ever be worthy,
Of the love we share.

Where does it all begin and where does it end

Where does it all begin and where does it end?
A sentimental journey, a death of a friend
The light shining far ahead, the road well trodden?
Wars past and present, bodies bloodstained and sodden?

Boundaries and borders, false and disputed,
Nations within nations, kingdoms agreed and refuted.
History written and untold, past down without discretion,
Opinions voiced in reckless genocide, slaughter following
obsession.

Communities from young to old, generation to generation,
Prisoners of past and present, birth and death their
celebration.
On and on the carnage surges, pointless yet always justifiable,
From the darkest part of mankind, the landscape of death
undeniable.

Centuries laid waste in time, empire upon empire,
With power over child or mother, a monumental funeral pyre.
Changes made in nation states, but not the hearts of one,
Can please a few and sometimes many, but what cost this
deed is done.

The voyeur with kaleidoscopic vision, drawn into despair and
destruction,
Can see and watch as politics with greed, turn power to
corruption.
Where does it all begin and where does it end, a sentimental,
journey the death of a friend?

Where is the Line

Where is the line between right and wrong?
Who are the unsung heroes?
Does faith come from within or from some far off mystical
place?
Is truth the goal of all human beings?
Or just a few sincere searchers?
Is love the foundation of the universe?
Or will the animal in man overpower the highest objectives?
Or will the unseen, unheard power of the creator sustain
forever man's need for wealth and power?
Is there life after death or just death in the midst of life?
Can the reality of all realities manifest itself and overcome
against all odds the darkest powers the negative side of
mankind?
Will peace be achieved in a lifetime of one single human being
Or is the search the goal and the ultimate meaning,
Just one step away?
Can sorrow be washed by time and grief fade with the opening
of new doors?
Will East meet West, the imbalance the injustices be cast to
the wind and total equality be achieved by all?
Will the wheels keep turning until the machinery or driving
forces finally break down and crumble,
Leaving the young the enlightened to forge a new?

Who has the most to say

An empty vessel makes the most sound.
Who has the most to say?
A nobody with something to say?
Or a somebody with nothing to say?
An empty vessel makes the most sound.

Within ourselves

We conclude where once we began,
With a breath.
All thoughts, actions and experiences have past by and are left
in a vacuum of none existence.
We are the sum of our life's experience.
Yet we are only as powerful as the breath that enters and
leaves our body.
We do not give breath, nor do we take it away.
We collide with life and life collides within us.
Spiralling on and on.
Until we meet ourselves.
Within ourselves.

Words in Waltz Time

Triplets of words, seven days a week,
Secretly, silently, seductively,
Defying the norm, outside of convention,
Bubbling, brimming, bursting.
Who is who, what is what,
Contemporary, contemptuously, constructed.
Thoughts on thoughts, deeds on deeds,
Momentously, movingly, moments,
Sections of seconds, scene on scene,
Potently, positively, passion.
Thrust of thirst, questions of questions,
Curiously, curiosity, culminates.
Rhythms on rhythms, sound on sound,
Percussively, proactively, performed.
Word after word, line on line,
Paragraphs, perfectly, punctuated.
Sonnets of songs, chapter and verse,
Eradicated, erotic, education.
Clause without claws, meaning without meaning,
Numerically, numbered, nothingness.
By popular demand, demanded by popularity,
Politics, politically, puerile.
Power without knowledge, knowledge without power,
Circling, circumventing, constitutions.
Death within life, life within death,
Cunningly, counterbalancing, conviction.
Stories of stories, tales of tales,
Generations, generally, gathering.
Foreplay to climax, beginning to end
Finally, fortuitously, finishes.

Your Birthday

Your birthday is special,
Though others may not always remember, you should never forget..
A celebration of the day you were born,
The moment of your first breath,
Life may not have been easy, no one ever said that it would,
But you have lived in a world filled with wonder and morning breaks every day.
So never forget your own birthday, the one day a year,
Mark it well.
Look forward with the eyes of a child and reflect with the mind of sage.
We don't know how many, may follow or how our health may fair.
So mark each birthday with something special, be with those who care.
Savour a day that is special, surrender to what may lay ahead.
You may share your birthdays with others by day, month or year,
But yours is your birthday, as your lifetime is your own,
The gifts you have received are especially for you,
The life you have is yours,
Use it well,
Use it wisely,
Love and be loved,
Care and be cared for,
Sing everyday,
Your birthday is special, a celebration,
The moment of your first breath.

Truth is universal, but our perception of it is individual.

Louisa Le Marchand 2008

More music CDs from Global Fusion Music & Arts

Farid Adjazairi 'RAl - Vibrant music from Algerian musician and composer Farid Adazairi capturing the spirit of the North African Berber culture.

GFMA-010

'Global Fusion World Music Compilation Volume 1', A collection of music from around the world as far afield as Japan, Grenada, India, Ireland, Uganda and much more.

GFMA-002

'Petals of passion' - A taste of India

GFMA - 003

'Tears of the Dragon' - A taste of the Far East

GFMA-004

'Ear of the Elephant' - A taste of Africa

GFMA-005